The Five Letters Every Christian Should Write

Reflections on Life, Death, and Spirit in the Age of Covid

David E. Gray

The Five Letters Every Christian Should Write: Reflections on Life, Death, and Spirit in the Age of Covid

ISBN: Softcover 978-1-951472-57-3

Copyright © 2020 by David E. Gray

All rights reserved. No part of this book may be reproduced or transmitted in any form or by any means, electronic or mechanical, including photocopying, recording, or by any information storage and retrieval system, without permission in writing from the publisher.

www.parsonsporch.com

*The Five Letters Every
Christian Should Write*

Acknowledgements

I give all gratitude to God, to Bridget for walking so many journeys with me, to our children for being so fun, and to the wonderful members of Bradley Hills Presbyterian Church for exploring these topics with me as we walk our journey together.

Contents

Acknowledgements 5
Prologue 9
Introduction 13
Chapter One 16
   Dealing with Our Grief in This Time 16
Chapter Two 27
   Letter Writing as a Spiritual Practice 27
Chapter Three 34
   A Letter to God 34
Chapter Four 41
   A Letter to Our Parents 41
Chapter Five 55
   A Letter to a Significant Person 55
Chapter Six 70
   A Letter to a Future Generation 70
Chapter Seven 95
   A Letter to Oneself 95
Conclusion 113

Prologue

This is a time like no other. As I write this, I sit at home, socially distant, sheltering in place, day after day, overwhelmed with oddity and yet trying to find the uniqueness of each 24-hour period. I have to remind myself what day it is in order not to miss appointments. Many of us are in our homes, where each day seems more similar to the last than different. It's quite a time.

Some in the public health field have said this is the most significant crisis the world has faced in more than fifty years. It is one of those rare times in history where everything seems to stop for a moment. Where time stands still. Where we know we will look back someday and ask each other, "Where were you when the Covid-19 pandemic hit?" Much like those in the past generations who asked similar questions about where they were on 9/11, or when the Challenger blew up or when JFK was shot. Where was I? What does it mean?

Most American, and many global, schools shut, for what would be the rest of the schoolyear, in March 2020. Businesses, churches, enterprises, restaurants, gyms, closed to in-person activities.

It feels like the whole world went on a retreat. We all began reflecting inwardly in relative isolation, whether we meant to or not. We began to wonder, when this ends, if it ends, how will the world emerge from it? Will we be different or the same?

We are all called to reflect on that question for ourselves and beyond. To use the retreat time that this is for personal, spiritual growth, if we can muster it. Henri Nouwen once said, "Solitude is the furnace of transformation."[1] What will change for you and for me from this time?

One of the most healthy spiritual practices a person can engage in is to put their feelings down on paper. This idea challenges me and I always learn something, gain a new perspective, when I put pen to paper. In an age of text messages, sound bites, emails, and short attention spans, actually taking the time to write out one's thoughts and feelings can be healthy. It also takes time. It is something I have long thought about doing in a systematic way, yet I found that in the busyness of my work and family life, I rarely have had the time to do it well. This Covid-retreat provides me what I've been missing – time. Perhaps to put pen to paper and actually write letters.

Writing this book has been a personal project, a spiritual practice that has allowed me to use the gift of relative retreat to put down "on paper" some of my own thoughts and feelings. Things I have been carrying around for a while. Writing these thoughts in the form of letters has been meaningful for me, not only to write in the present, but, I hope, to be able to look back later on, and in some cases, share.

The invitation of this work is for us to write letters as a personal spiritual act. To take advantage of this unusual time to put down on paper our thoughts and feelings specifically in a series of letters. To deepen our relationship with God through penning letters. Perhaps to open new avenues of communication with others.

For many of us, this could be a very personal experience of sharing what is not easily articulated to ourselves or to

---

[1] For more on this wisdom, see Henri Nouwen. *The Way of the Heart: Connecting with God through Prayer, Wisdom and Silence.* Ballantine Books Revised and ed. edition, 2003.

others or to God. The act of making those private thoughts and feelings even a bit more public, that is, putting them "down on paper," and sharing them with another human being or God or to face them ourselves, requires courage in some cases.

It can allow the Holy Spirit to come afresh for us as well. Such actions can begin a healthy spiritual practice, which, I hope for me, and perhaps for you too, lasts long after a vaccine for coronavirus is found or this Covid-retreat ends.

While this book is written with Christian allusions and references, the spiritual practice of letter writing is just as valuable for Jews, Muslims, members of Eastern faiths or any religion, or those with no faith tradition. As such, this book may have resonance with a broader group of readers, for everyone can benefit from the practice of writing letters.

Many religions help people find real meaning in life, but as a Christian, I write this from the perspective of a follower of Jesus Christ. Thus, there is much of this work that is informed by a Christian mindset and my training and experience as a parish pastor.

For Christians, the season of Lent is the 40-day period in the church calendar which encourages inward reflection to prepare for the celebration of Easter. Some say that this Covid retreat time, which began in Lent 2020, is an "extended Lent," in which we have no choice but to stay home and, with so much else canceled, to focus inwards. Perhaps we might embrace this opportunity to write letters then and to see where it leads.

As I write this, America has passed 125,000 deaths from Covid-19. Many of us are reflecting on life and death. This is a time of great tragedy. So many of us have lost someone, or been ill ourselves, or feel vulnerable emotionally, spiritually, financially or mentally scared at this time. Many have lost a job, or seen plans change. Many have watched school end prematurely or graduation ceremonies altered. Some of us have seen dreams die.

Letter writing can help us address our feelings about this serious time. Perhaps making it a sacred time. For this reason, we'll end each chapter with a prayer to God.

I suggest that at some point in our lives, everyone should write letters, including these five letters suggested here. There may be no better time to write them than now. Writing them may help us deal with the past, live in the present, and prepare for the future. We may ask ourselves:

What is our spiritual core? What do we believe about God? How do we feel about our parents? What do we need to let go of about a significant other? How do we say thank you to a teacher or mentor? What are our beliefs about life and death? What legacy would we like to leave for the future? How do we make sense of this particular time? What does it take for us to move forward in it? What goals do we hope to set for ourselves? Where do we find meaning in this time? Where do we find holiness in it?

I began this project to answer some of these questions for myself. This work has helped me, but I am a work in progress. Perhaps you may use this retreat time to answer some of those questions for yourself too. With God's help, may it be so. Amen.

Introduction

On March 1, 2020, I led worship at Bradley Hills Presbyterian Church as usual. I finished the last hymn of the worship service, I delivered the benediction, and recessed down the aisle out the door. As I waited to shake the many hands that would pass by me heading out of the sanctuary, our head usher for the day asked me, "Are you prepared to cancel worship soon?"

"What are you talking about?" I asked him back. I could not image what the future would soon hold. I couldn't conceive that not only worship, but much of life, would soon be cancelled or postponed. How right he turned out to be.

The following Monday I received a text, "This thing is much more serious than what everyone is letting on, more than what the media is reporting. Take it seriously. Be cautious."

The first time I got a gulp in my throat from thinking about the virus was when that friend texted. This was a person with access to more detailed specifics than I was aware of. He worked closely with many in government and was worried about what he had been told by colleagues about the seriousness of the virus.

Soon the church, the state, the nation, the world, began to shut down. Two weeks later, we were meeting virtually as a church. Schools began to close, something I could not have imagined. Shaking hands would become a thing of the past. Worship with large numbers would be on hold. We would be entering a new world.

I started getting notes from friends who would become ill with the virus. A dear friend in Pennsylvania who had mild symptoms and who recovered, but worried about infecting his parents. A good friend closer by, whose restaurants our family appreciates, having a case, and several family members, though not all of his nuclear family, turned out to be asymptomatic carriers. Friends from New York who had serious illnesses. Some from the West coast who traveled widely, but then feared for their lives. Acquaintances on ventilators, and dear ones scared. For a while in late March, I was afraid to turn on the news or look at Facebook because it seemed that every moment, someone else I knew was developing symptoms. Testing was scarce so others weren't sure if they had the virus. Many were confused and scared.

At the same time, my mother-in-law was quarantined in our basement as she made it on one of the last flights out of Europe at a critical time in mid-March when the disease was spreading there. For two weeks we barely saw her as she braved the challenge of not knowing if she would become ill. My own parents were in the midst of moving from the home they had resided in for 45 years so were in frequent contact with a variety of people, making distancing challenging.

In our circles, we had several friends who were doctors and nurses on the front lines of hospital emergency rooms and were feeling overwhelmed with cases and underwhelmed by the lack of Personal Protective Equipment. We made masks for local hospitals as a church community and prayed in gratitude for those first responders. In our congregation, friends emailed me for prayers for chills they were experiencing. One who tested positive and had children to care for. Friends who were now sick.

Then people at the church I served became ill. A friend I had traveled with went from seeming to be fine one morning to seeing oxygen levels dropping quickly to dying early the next morning.

Due to the deaths from Covid and other diseases, funerals began to be backlogged. By the end of May we had nine families who wanted memorial services, but had to wait because we were not allowed to have more than ten people in the sanctuary at a time. We discussed holding virtual funerals over Zoom. I conducted a burial where I stood next to a casket and a computer with family members sitting in their cars nearby watching on the phones. I stood in sanctuary columbariums with the adult children of the deceased in masks watching as I conducted an inurnment service for a loved one. One for a dear friend now missing her husband. I have dear friends who still, as I write this, are waiting to have a chance to plan a fitting and meaningful memorial service.

This is a deeply emotional time. A time where we are trying to make sense of our emotions, our thoughts, and the challenges we face. A time when we are perhaps searching for ways to make sense of the deep grief we are experiencing. A time when we are looking for ways to process the pain and uncertainty.

Letter writing might be a way for us to confront, address and deal with our grief of what has been, and is being, lost in this time. It might strengthen our spirit. Let me suggest there are five letters every Christian should consider writing during their lifetime. They may be particularly helpful to write during this Covid-time, as we work through our emotions of this experience.

Chapter One
Dealing with Our Grief in This Time

Experiencing Grief

Whatever happens during this Covid-distancing time, whether we "return to normal" soon through an earlier than predicted vaccine or therapy, or if the displacement takes a long time, we are grieving. Wherever you and those you love are during this time, I hope you and yours are ok, learning and growing from this most challenging time.

For those of us reading this in later years, "after-Covid," may this serve as a kind of diary to mark what happened and give insights for future generations on what we experienced during this unusual time.

The theme which I hear most of all now from this Covid time, from a variety of sources, is grief.

I have had several occasions where I have had to counsel people about some very serious situations they are facing this spring. Yet I've had to do that over a technology I had barely heard of but has become all the rage - Zoom. I didn't think I would be counseling anyone over Zoom anytime ever, but here I find myself.

This is a disorienting time. It's like the world has gone on a retreat. Part silent, part talking. We are in a time of relative solitude. Some of us are super busy being teachers and parents and workers. Others have a lot of free time, too much, and feel isolated. Some of us have lost a job or gotten sick or have a loved-one ill. For some of us, we relish this time of reflection. Others love the daily programs of life, including the church, as a part of dealing with the isolation, and want more. Some of us like parts of this time better than the way many things used to be. I know several of us that like the relative quiet of this time. Others find this highly disruptive and overwhelming. People are at differing places in some ways.

Yet nearly everyone I've talked with is dealing with some level of grief. Those who are bored and those who are overwhelmed are both grieving something. Many of us are grieving deeply. Even if we ourselves haven't lost something, at very least we grieve for losses in our broader community and world. Most of us are concerned about someone in our family or friend system now. More Americans have already died in a short time from the virus than died during the entire Vietnam War. The former head of the CDC, Tom Frieden, wrote in the Washington Post in May 14, 2020, that none of us are unscathed by grief.[2] As we move through stages of grief, we have to be gracious with ourselves and each other and try to accept where we are.[3]

We are grieving. We have lost lives and financial security and school time and plans and hope. A March 23, 2020 article in the Harvard Business Review got my attention.[4] It's not every day that the Harvard Business Review talks about grief. Yet in it, Scott Berinato quoted David Kessler, who worked closely with Elisabeth Kübler-Ross, and who argued that

---

[2] Tom Frieden. "We Need to Enter the Fifth Stage of Coronavirus Grief: Acceptance. *Washington Post.* May 14, 2020; https://www.washingtonpost.com/opinions/2020/05/14/we-need-enter-fifth-stage-coronavirus-grief-acceptance/.

[3] Ibid.

[4] Scott Berinato. "That Discomfort You're Feeling is Grief." Harvard Business Review. March 23, 2020; https://hbr.org/2020/03/that-discomfort-youre-feeling-is-grief.

ultimately, we can survive our grief in this time by finding meaning in it.[5]

How do we find meaning during this time? During a dry time, a time where we find ourselves between a rock and a hard place, where do we find water in the rock to help us deal with the grief? In support of my congregation, I tried to compile resources for this particular time of grief, retreat, and loss. I have been trying to read books on grace and dying, and on solitude, as well as classic literature on the subjects. What resources have you found helpful to find meaning out of this time?

I think about the biblical Book of Exodus and how God helped Moses draw water from a rock when the Israelites were in a wilderness time too. How do we draw water out of rocks? Make lemonade out of lemons. Find silver linings.[6] Think of this retreat time as one to help you find meaning.

Grief Flowing from "Bad Things" in the World

We experience grief as a natural reaction when things seem negative. When we have lost something, or are sad, we often experience grief. The grief we feel flows from the bad things that happen in our world.

During this time, some of us sit at our home office desks and stare out the window. Something is gnawing at our heart. Some thought is keeping us from concentrating on our work. The worries cloud our minds. We wonder when a break to this distancing will come. When a respite will occur.

---

5 Ibid.

6 For more about silver linings, see TheBigThing.org.

We try and move towards some other thought. We long for the gift of concentration. The worries of the day can morph into the nightmares of night.

We are concerned about things in our world. We read the newspapers. We try and make sense of this situation. We watch the news. The questions of our lives flow forward, and we ask the difficult questions of why this virus and those economic hardships and these injustices seem to be happening in our world.

We continue to worry about the losses of our lives, and the suffering of our world at this time. We look around and see the pain of the world and wonder why such pain occurs. Why doesn't God enter in directly to change it? Where is God at this time? Do you ever feel that way? I do. This is the question the Israelites asked Moses in the wilderness of Sinai when they were hungry and thirsty. This is the question Job asked when he faced terrible trials. It is the question even Jesus asked on the cross, wondering if God had forsaken him.

I had a call with a friend recently who is undergoing a significant physical challenge. The person shared their story of treatment during this time and progress and yet also their complications and disappointment.

The person called their condition the "unwanted visitor." An illness and situation we didn't ask for, but which we now experience.

This virus is an unwanted visitor.

We all have had moments where we cry in our own way with the Psalmist, "My soul is cast down within me….and I say to God, 'Why have you forgotten me?' Why must I walk about mournfully because the enemy oppresses me?"

My friend asked, "Why does God give us such pain and challenge? Why does God allow me to have this unwanted visitor?"

My own sense of God is that God doesn't punish us with pain and virus and challenge.

God created our world and is ultimately in control. I affirm that God is all powerful. Our hymns sing of Gods glory. Scripture tells us God is in charge of the world. Our observation of the planet shows us that there must be something out there to make our complex universe.

God knows us. The one whom the Psalms and the prophets affirm numbers our hairs, understands us completely, and sends a spirit of guidance, is all knowing.

God loves us.

Yet God limits God's own power. God so loves the world that God comes into it in Christ. In coming as a man in Jesus and later even through the Holy Spirit, the infinite God limited Godself to our time and space. Jesus' allowing himself to be captured and crucified, and God choosing the trinity as the way to be expressed to us rather than, say, more additional parts to the Godhead, are examples of God limiting Godself.

The result of God limiting Godself is that God gives us freedom. We get to make choices. Decisions about how to act and what to do.

Yet in limiting Godself so as to give us freedom, God allows chaos and bad things like viruses to be in the world.

At the beginning, the world was a chaotic, formless void. The word for formless means chaotic. In the creation narrative of Genesis 1, we read that God brought order to chaos, but didn't eliminate chaos. As we economically develop our planet, we uncover viruses which risk new diseases. The circle of life on a planet with limited resources allows for death, truly the final frontier, yet we grieve in the process.

Expressing Our Grief During the Challenge of Viral Times

There is good in the world because God loves the world. So much as to send God's son. In Emmanuel, Jesus, God came into our midst to suffer along with us, to care for us and to show us what it means to choose love. Christ is our wanted visitor, our needed visitor, our holy visitor.

St. Matthew tells us that the last words Jesus spoke as recorded in his Gospel are, "Know I am with you always until the end of the age."

We can hear that voice when we are facing an unwanted visitor. When we stare out the window asking "why?" We hear the voice of the savior coming into our lives. As we look in disbelief at our TV's or read the newspapers. As we get the unwanted phone call or text. We receive the voice saying through the spirit, "I will never leave you or forsake you or give up on you. Have faith, courage and hope." God saying, "Let me be the wanted visitor who goes along with you. For I will help guide your feet, hold your hand, and lead you home."

One of the best pieces of advice I have ever gotten is that when facing a challenge, don't hold in all your emotions, picture the worst-case scenario in your mind, and express your grief. If you can come to terms with the worst-case scenario, you will be ok, whatever happens. I can't recall who first gave that advice to me, but whenever I have followed it, it has made a difference for me. It has helped calm me in anxious moments and has given some confidence and courage.

Julia of Norwich knew about challenging times. She was a mystic in the 14th century and experienced great grief. She experienced the black plague in which bacteria brought by fleas on rats entered Europe and killed millions. Her reflection on suffering during a time of the spread of disease led her to experience the revelation of God's divine love. Julia was on her deathbed dealing with deep grief. She thought the end was near. Then in her grief, she felt the love of Jesus coming towards her. She concluded that God was love and all that we are to focus on is love. She expressed her feelings in perhaps the oldest surviving literature written in English by a female, her *Revelation of Divine Love.*[7]

That is the opportunity of this time too. Our perspective is changed. At church, we are looking at worshiping God in new ways. Online, virtually, at home. We are used to being in the sanctuary. We are used to sitting in a particular row. Now we watch on a screen. The music sounds different. The pastor sounds different. The look and feel of worship are different.

What will we learn in this time? What one friend called a "reset of what is most important." Things are be done differently in it and some things will be done differently coming out of it.

What is the new perspective you will gain on God or life or yourself? A new perspective can help you find meaning and deal with the grief.

Perhaps we will conclude, as Julia of Norwich did, that whatever we do and whatever meaning we find in this time, it must start with and be guided by the love of God. It is the love of God which will help us express our grief during this time.

---

[7] Julia of Norwich. *Revelations of Divine Love.* 14th century.

That is what Jesus teaches too. Think about the courage of Jesus on Holy Week. Scholars have long debated about whether or not Jesus was afraid before his death. Literature and songs have argued both sides. Yet, the Bible tells us that, as with our lives, Jesus probably had mixed emotions. On one hand, the Bible never says directly that Jesus is afraid, it doesn't use the word for fear, *phobos,* for Jesus. He shows little fear during his trial or with Pilate. He seems almost calm at times on the cross. When women were weeping for him, he said, "Daughters of Jerusalem, do not weep for me...."

Yet when Jesus took Peter and James and John with him, he looked sorrowful and distressed. Jesus said to his disciples, "My soul is grieved even to the point of death" and "Now my soul is troubled." Luke records Jesus as saying, "I have a baptism to be baptized with, and how distressed I am till it is accomplished." Such statements of anxiety in several different Gospels reveal a Jesus who was anxious at times. Jesus knew what was going to happen to him as he entered Jerusalem on Palm/Passion Sunday. Jesus predicted his betrayal and death. Jesus was fully human as well as fully divine. Jesus felt for people. He sympathized with them. He felt pity for them. When his friend, Lazarus died, Jesus wept. So, it should not surprise us that the author of the Book of Hebrews writes, "During the last days of Jesus' life on earth, he offered up prayers and petitions with loud cries and tears to the one who could save him from death." On the cross on Good Friday, Jesus would yell *"Eloi, Eloi, lama sabachthani"* - "My God, My God why has though forsaken me." The Gospels and Hebrews describe Jesus as full of and expressing real, honest emotions, including strong anxiety, when he entered Jerusalem knowing what would come next, and as he approached death.

Jesus lived during a key point in the history of Greek stoicism, a philosophy that taught that by training the mind one can free oneself from passions and reduce fear and suffering. Yet Jesus chose to express those emotions during and around Holy Week. Jesus' display of emotion reinforces his humanity and vulnerability. It makes it clear to us that God has chosen to be with us. This matters because it helps us affirm that if Jesus can express honest emotions in the face of challenge, so we can. So, when we face something difficult and we are afraid, as we all are at times, we are in good company. The best imaginable.

Courage is not having no fears. Courage in continuing on the path despite them. When you think of courageous people, who do you think of? Dietrich Bonhoeffer? Martin Luther King, Jr? Gandhi? Rosa Parks? They expressed their grief and fear when acting in the face of oppression but went forward anyway.

In Gethsemane, at a critical moment in Holy Week, Jesus felt overwhelmed, sorrowful, and troubled, to the point of death. He asked God in prayer if there was another way where he didn't have to suffer. He understood what was coming. He was not stoic but full of the same emotions any of us would experience. Then he said to God, "Not as I will, but as you will." He stood his ground. Just as he walked into the heart of the empire, Jesus' passion for God's kingdom gave him courage to continue through the city and through Holy Week. Matthew tells us that in the garden, Jesus returned to his disciples and found them sleeping. Clearly frustrated he said, "Couldn't you men keep watch with me for one hour?" You can almost hear him going back to God saying, "Ok, these guys aren't going to protect me, I really need your help God." Jesus prayed a second time to God, asking if the cup could be taken from him, but again said, "May your will be done." All awhile his disciples couldn't even stay awake to help him. Their failed discipleship reinforced that Jesus was on his own. Then a third time he prayed the same thing; he wished for another path but was willing to continue on it to do God's will. Courage can be realizing what is before you, that sometimes we seem to be isolated, even alone in one's house, walking alone, but trusting God enough in prayer to be able to continue on the path.

When do you pray most fervently? Before you go into surgery? While a family member undergoes a test? As someone you know heads abroad in service of their country? After you go into that tough meeting with a boss? Before you open the letter from a college admissions department? Before you listen to that answering machine message from someone you'd like to call a friend? When you are grieving something deeply?

Have you been praying during this Covid time? This is a fearful time.

We realize there are times when we all walk great paths of challenge. We all can be anxious.

You may find that the closer you get to God, the more you find yourself motivated by courage and hope, rather than fear. God is not far away, but near. God is with as we bear our cross. As we walk through the valley of the shadow of death.

When we say, "the Lord be with you," and "also with you," as many churches during communion, we affirm that God is with us even in our grief and fears. For even if all that you have and rely on goes away, you are still loved by God. If you can picture that worst-case scenario and you can end up realizing you are loved by God, you will have courage for the journey.

This is a tough time for more of us. We don't need to sugar coat life, hide our fear, or bury our passion during Covid. Jesus didn't. See things as they are with all their challenge and complexity. Be who you are. For who you are beautiful to God, just as you are.

Let Jesus hold you in your grief. So that you may express how you feel.

The realities of life, accidents and aging, mistakes and mortality, disease and shortcomings, challenges of Covid-19, are still here even if we have faith. But we get through them together when we have faith. Together is where we belong when the storm hits. With our friends. With our church. With our families.

This is a unique time of storms for us with the virus. Allow Christ to be with your solitude, your fear, your grief of this time. Picture the worst-case scenario. Confront your grief. Don't be afraid to express yourself within it. Have the courage to express your grief.

Then pick up a pen and write about it.

Chapter Two
Letter Writing as a Spiritual Practice

I have found that one helpful way to express one's feelings, including grief, is to write down what one feels. Perhaps letter writing can be a meaningful spiritual practice for you during the grief of this Covid time.

Spiritual Practices

During the plagues of the 14th century, Julia of Norwich reportedly developed a four part "body prayer" to help her cope with the suffering and grief. In it she lifted up the idea that we should "await for God's presence, allow God's presence to come or not, accept that we are not in control and attend to God's love and calling in the world."[8] These practices helped her deal with her grief. They have helped me during this time too.

During this most unusual time, if love and meaning are our goals, we need spiritual practices. Spiritual practices are gifts from God.

We are in a world of social distancing. Of quarantine. Or being apart. We are inside, or away from so many things we are used to. We have more time alone, and more solitude. How do we fill the time? I have never been more convinced of the importance of faith in helping us respond and deal with this time than right now. These are times when we may have to do the individual work of spiritual practices to make it through.

How can facing Covid-19 can change one's spirituality? One way is by making each moment more precious. As I've talked with friends and parishioners and others who have

---

8 Ibid, Attributed to Julia of Norwich in the 14th century.

survived, they say this time makes each moment matter more. It can make the most important things in life seem bigger.

This past winter, our family went to the Washington Capitals professional hockey game. I love watching sports live. Yet, I'm not sure when we can return to that. We were there to see a famous Capitals player, a player with number 8. One of our clan looked at his jersey and asked why we was cheering for "Ovi-chicken." They meant Washington star Alex Ovechkin, who scored once, his 699th all-time goal, while we were there.

As we watched the game, between the periods all the Washington and Montreal players came off the ice. After a while, a machine called a Zamboni came on to smooth the ice. It was like a big buffer and my kids liked seeing it.

At one point during the rest period, with all the regular players in the locker room, there was an entertaining school-age game on the ice where two teams of elementary school age kids got to play a 5-minute exhibition game. One of our own young children, who had been in the bathroom when the Caps and the other team, the Canadians, players went to the locker room, came back and, watching part of the kid's exhibition hockey game, asked, "How did all the players get so much smaller?"

The ice, the rink, the puck was the same, but what we came to see, where the action was, what really mattered to the kids, the players, seemed suddenly a lot smaller.

Many of us find ourselves in a place where we ask, "How did the stuff that matters get so much smaller in my life?"

We used to be excited about purpose, about activities, about living with excitement for many parts of our journey.

Yet somewhere along the way, what is most meaningful in life became smaller as our commitments, obligations, routines, took over. Where did all the time go?

Or during Covid-isolation, so much of what we prize is distant.

How did everything that really matters to us get so much smaller?

This unusual season could be, however, a time to make some of the other things in life matter more.

Perhaps, for people wanting to go deeper in finding meaning in life, our spiritual practices can loom larger during this time.

Writing as a Such a Practice

The practice of letter writing may have new value during this time.

Devotionally, and as I pray, I have been thinking about a desire to write more letters. Letter writing is a lost art. Before computers, handwritten notes were the standard. That was how so many of us communicated. Now, emails have largely replaced handwritten notes. Emails are certainly fine, yet perhaps in the computer era, handwritten notes are even more unique and special now to write and receive.

Meaningful writing emerged from what is known in the Bible as the Exile experience of the Israelites. From around 597BC-530 BC, many of those who had lived in Judah were in exile in Babylon. This was a period when much of the Hebrew Bible was formed, when it actually came together. The 39 books of the Old Testament first were oral stories told from generation to generation, then were mixed together with written records, and then collected and edited by multiple authors.

These books weren't organized until the Exile. Until the time of isolation and being separated, then the Israelites wrote down in the canon, the stories of their people, in one place, one larger book. They needed them in their isolation more than ever to survive.

So do we. A silver lining in a difficult time. Perhaps we will write down our stories during this time too.

Theologian Henry Nouwen, once said, "Writing can be a true spiritual discipline. Writing can help us…. get in touch with the deeper stirrings of our hearts…Writing can become lifesaving for us and sometimes for others too."[9]

What spiritual practices do we use or lean into to make the most out of this solitude time?   Rediscovering the art of letter writing can be a spiritual practice that may be helpful. Let me suggest that we learn from the letters of the New Testament.

Letter writing seems to have gone out of style. In the age of email and texts, fewer of us communicate by letter than in the past. Yet I know that many continue to value letter writing. I appreciate the letters of parishioners.

For years, my grandmother had what she called "a round robin letter" with eleven good friends from the Northwestern University class of 1929. They had a group of twelve handwritten letters which were constantly in circulation as friends would update each other on their lives. The packet would arrive to each person about once a year. A person would take their old letter out, write a new one, and mail the package to the next person. It took about a month for each person to write and send the package, so annually my grandmother would get a new package. From

---

[9] Henri Nouwen in https://henrinouwen.org/meditation/writing-save-day/.

there she would read the other eleven letters and write her new one. Twelve good friends writing letters to each other.

One could see the twelve disciples appreciating communicating together like that.

As we see, one Biblical character for whom letter writing was particularly important was the Apostle Paul.

The Letters of Paul

Letter writing is central to the Bible. The majority of the New Testament is comprised of the letters of an early Christian named Paul. The Apostle Paul was a religious Pharisee who rejected and, indeed, persecuted, Christians, early in his career. Then Jesus came to him on a road towards Damascus and he began the life of following Jesus and proclaiming his saving acts on a series of journeys. Paul's life was one of stark contrasts. He went from chief persecutor to chiefly persecuted. He first rejected, then embraced, then explained, the Christian faith.

Paul wrote letters himself to early churches to help explain the faith. He depended on the openness and hospitality of those we visited.

There is much we could argue about regarding Paul. I appreciate his faith, his use of language, and his ability to proclaim the Gospel in ways that spoke and speak to particular and changing contexts. He would reach out to specific churches to speak to the context of his day and the issues people were facing.

The most common type of literature in the New Testament are the 13 letters written by the Apostle Paul. Scholars will debate which letters were actually written by Paul (somewhere between 7 and 14) but each show wisdom and help the reader draw closer to the holy in life.

Paul didn't write these letters as leisurely reflections on the world. Most of the letters were serious business. They were written to argue for faith in Christ. Or to correct inaccurate belief. Or to push or to explain and teach. They were written to specific, fledgling churches throughout Asia Minor struggling to understand and grow and thrive in a hostile world.

Paul's ministry was one that fundamentally opened up Christianity from being a small Jewish sect to becoming a rapidly growing ministry among the gentiles to being one which spread to all corners of the world.

Each of these letters shows something personal for and about Paul. In some letters Paul defends his ministry. In some he writes tenderly to a followers or group of disciples. In each, Paul writes with hopes as to friends. In Paul's letters, he seeks to make a difference, but also to share something of himself. He writes, inspired by the spirit, in a way that perhaps was helpful to him as well as to the recipients.

Letter writing, at its best, can be helpful to those of us writing, as well as the recipient of letters.

So, let me suggest that as faithful people, as Christians, and as all who seek a spiritual life, we try and write five letters.

Throughout this work, we will seek to rediscover the ancient practice of writing letters as a spiritual practice.

We will do so by looking at portions of several of Paul's letters in each chapter that follows as inspiration for our own.

There are many scriptures that will be helpful to our journey together and will be lifted up in this work, from the Gospels and Hebrew Bible, in addition to those letters written by Paul, though Paul's words will be a main focus of each section.

We will end each of our five chapters on the five letters with a prayer as well, to remind ourselves to connect to the source of all holiness in the universe.

When I was writing a draft of this work and was going to introduce Paul, I spellchecked a draft. I put in the word, "Apostle," but spelled it just off so that spellcheck came back with the word "post office." Perhaps as we read from the New Testament letters of Paul, we can picture Paul sending/mailing his letters to churches in his day. Perhaps then we should think about writing and mailing our own letters.

I have Muslim friends who pray five times a day. The actions of prayer five times are an act of connecting frequently with God. Muslims also make a special trip, a pilgrimage, Hajj, once in their lifetimes. In a related way, I think that over the lifetime of every Christians, there are five letters we should consider writing. If we are able to do so, such acts can draw us closer to God.

There are many letters that a person could write that they might find meaningful. We don't have the ability to write to everyone. Some of us are busier now than before this crisis. Yet I believe that in writing a letter to God, a letter to our parents, a letter to a significant other, a letter to the next generation and a letter to ourselves, we may clarify our thoughts, find calm in anxious times, develop a healthy spiritual habit, and rediscover some of the holiness of God in this most unusual social distancing time.

Chapter Three
A Letter to God

One of the best-known stories involving the Apostle Paul is his conversion in Acts 9, when Jesus confronted him on the road to Damascus and he became Christ's follower. I picture Paul sitting on a chair in a dark room in Damascus a few days later, writing a letter to God, trying to make sense of what he has gone through and thanking God in Christ for coming to him and changing his life. As we explore the letters of Paul, beginning with his first letter to the church at Corinth, we realize how important writing was to this complex person.

As we think about letter writing as a spiritual discipline, we might begin by writing a letter to God, the source of all life and a very personal recipient.

Approaching God

Paul wrote to the church at Corinth in what would be modern-day Greece. It was a church which had lost focus on the most important things, where God had become small compared to how members were spending their time.

Paul wrote a portion of 1 Corinthians to summarize his faith. That Christ had died and rose from the dead and appeared to many people.

Paul expresses that faith is of "first importance." It is a most important thing. Paul was calling upon the Corinthians to make their relationship with God and its expression a more central part of their lives.

By reflecting on the place of God in your life and addressing God in a letter, perhaps you will find that God takes on a bigger role in your life.

I love the recent story I heard told several times about a hockey player named David Ayers. As I understand it, Ayers used to play hockey regularly as a goalie until an injury in 2004 ended his career. Yet he still loved being around hockey. So much so that he had a job as Director of Operations at the Mattamy Athletic Center in Toronto, where one of his responsibilities is driving the Zamboni machines to buffer the ice between periods at the stadium where the Toronto Maple Leaves professional hockey team played. One day, the Carolina Hurricanes were in town playing Toronto. Well, first Carolina's starting goalie got hurt. Then in the second period, their backup goals got injured. They were on the road. They needed someone to play goalie. So, in the middle of the game, they recalled the 42-year-old, Ayers to take off his Zamboni gloves and put on a hockey uniform and play goalie for them. He was nervous at first and gave up two goals. His teammates reportedly said, "Don't worry…have fun with it." At crunch time, Ayers saved eight crucial shots in a row to save the win for Carolina, who was fighting for a playoff spot. He earned himself a lot of interviews, including a spot on the Stephen Colbert show, and was made an honorary Carolinian by the governor. A most unlikely hero, an unexpected person, came out to save the day.

The Apostle Paul was an unlikely hero too. A person who at one time was less than kind to Christians, was called to articulate the faith by writing letters in which he reflected his experience with God. He reflected on God's love for him by writing to the Corinthians and other churches about how they could make God a larger part of their lives.

We often think we are not worthy to approach God. Indeed, we are not. Yet that should not stop us. For Christ came so that we could approach God. Jesus lived and died so that we need not be afraid of anything in the world.

Because Jesus came into the world, we can approach the throne of God with confidence.

Because Jesus died and rose, your sins and mine no longer separate us from God. As Paul wrote to the Roman church, nothing separates us from the love of God.

What do you believe about God? Perhaps consider approaching God with your views. Have confidence, have courage, have fun, and have at it – write a letter to God in whatever form you'd like. On a napkin, on stationary, on a piece of lined paper.

Two of the most helpful ways I have found to write a letter to God are 1) simply to write a prayer and 2) writing a statement of faith.

Write a Prayer

What does it mean to write a letter to God?

There are parts of Paul's letter to the Corinthians which read like a prayer. In them, we can hear Paul almost pleading with the Corinthians to remember what he told them. Paul's strong reminders are often like prayers. When he wants something so much for someone in his letters, he almost expresses his concern like a prayer.

In many ways, prayer is like a letter to God. When we pray to God, praying is like articulating a personal letter to an old friend. Sometimes it's a prayerful letter of gratitude. Other times our prayers are like a letter of anger or of questioning. Perhaps your prayers are like a letter asking for help for oneself or one we love.

When we pray with the children at the end of the children's message in our worship services at my church or at night, we often begin by saying, "Dear God," and the kids repeat "Dear God." Like a letter.

There is no spiritual practice that connects us more deeply into relationship with God than prayer. Prayer is adoration, confession, thanksgiving, and supplication or whatever is authentic and personal to us.

So, our first invitation of writing a letter to God is to pray to God early and often. To deepen our relationship with God. To practice composing a letter to God when we pray.

Write a Statement of Faith

Our second invitation is to write a letter to God by penning what is called a statement of faith. That is, a brief summary of what we believe.

In a portion 1 Corinthians 15, Paul writes what has been called by some to be a statement of faith. He summarizes his belief about the Christian faith that Christ died and rose and appeared, arguing for a focus on God.

When I became a pastor, I had to write a statement of my own faith to be approved by those examining me. I began mine so many years ago by writing, "With humility and excitement, I respond to God's initiation of faith in my life. I have experienced God's grace in good times and in bad, and trust that the God who delivered the Israelites from exile and pulled Paul from his path, is the God who sustains me, who saves me for Christ's sake, and who calls me to service."

Then I proceeded to write out what I believed about God as a statement to connect me more deeply to my creator.

As I presented mine, I was nervous, as putting my personal beliefs down "on paper" was one thing, but when one becomes a pastor one has those beliefs dissected by a variety of people. At one meeting about them, I took a number of challenging questions about the verb tense I was using in my statement.

When our young people join a church such as mine, they confirm the baptismal vows their parents made by claiming and affirming their own faith. They do so by presenting an articulation of what they believe through writing what is called a statement of their faith.

When our boards of directors, new elders, and deacons, are elected, they write statements of faith to present to become officers of the church.

In our Presbyterian Book of Confessions, we have many statements of faith. Such as the 1983 "Brief Statement of Faith" we often read in worship.

I don't think one needs to "present" their statement to have a meaningful spiritual experience. A statement of faith begins with something personal. It can stay that way.

Writing a statement of faith can be a most meaningful spiritual practice for this time. When I speak with officers of the church in the weeks after the write a statement of faith, they often state that writing the statement of faith was one of the most meaningful spiritual activities they have ever engaged in. I believe that is true for me. It was far less important what anyone else thinks, than what one takes from the experience of putting pen to paper or fingers to keyboard and writing a prayerful statement to God.

Try writing a letter to God in which you articulate what it is you believe. Where are you now on your journey of faith? Putting pen to paper and expressing what you believe forces you to slow down, to reflect on God, perhaps to wrestle with doubt, and to articulate what you feel. Try it in a form that is personal, like you are writing to a friend.

What is it you believe about God? What are your questions and uncertainty? Who and what has nurtured your faith? How do you celebrate it each day? What do you believe about God, Jesus, and the Holy Spirit? What are your gifts and how will you use them to deepen your relationship with God this Covid-retreat time, so that the things that really matter take a bigger role in your life?

Put this letter aside and read it the next month or in a year later and see how your views and statement have changed.

The Apostle Paul was a most unlikely hero. An unexpected person to save the Corinthians. Paul writes that the Gospel is what will save the frustrated, adrift, myopic Corinthians. That a relationship with God can help focus one on a more meaningful life now and pave the way to eternal life with Christ. Paul believed articulating faith could help save the Corinthians.

Yet because of what he had done previously in rejecting God and God's people and what he had left undone, Paul felt unworthy to express his faith. He said he didn't deserve to be an apostle. The word apostle has two meanings. It can mean the original twelve who followed Jesus. Paul was not one of those twelve. Its second meaning is to be one of many messengers of faith. Paul meant that he was not worthy to be one of the many other people who were apostles in that they expressed or articulated their faith to someone else. Yet he was called to articulate it.

Expressing our faith is not easy. Articulating what we believe, including our questions and doubts, our hopes, and dreams, does not come naturally to many of us. We may feel unworthy to express our faith to God. Yet the grace available to Paul is available to us.

Try a personal letter between you and God. Don't worry too much about its format. This is your moment, have fun with it. God is waiting to receive your letter.

It doesn't matter who you are or what you have done or left undone in the past; this could be a time to consider a new direction.

It doesn't matter how you write to God, whether by praying or writing a statement of faith, or some other expression you come up with, consider writing to God.

If everything else we have been investing time in in life doesn't satisfy, the call of this Covid season could be to recall your spiritual life, which might be what unexpectedly saves you this season.

Prayer

Loving God, give us the courage to reflect, recall and express how we feel, to address and confront, and to work through our feelings of this time, by writing a letter to you. That our faith might be renewed. So that we might have a closer walk with thee. Amen.

Chapter Four

A Letter to Our Parents

On March 9, 2020, my parents and I drove to dinner in Dayton, Ohio. We found a lucky parking spot on Brown St. and walked into the familiar door of the Pine Club, one of my favorite places to dine. We sat in a familiar booth with similar people around as I was used to seeing there. We had a familiar meal without a lot of anxiety.

One week later that restaurant and all the others in Ohio were closed. Anxiety was everywhere. It was hard to fly anywhere for a time. It was such an amazing change of events. I am grateful for that time I had with my parents before things "shut down," and travel became more difficult.

I give thanks for my parents, for so many things, including for modeling going to church, and for thinking about things of the spirit. Parenting can be difficult, but it also can be a spiritual practice.

Everything around us and inside us seems to be impacted by this Covid time. Covid-19 forces us to reflect on our mortality. This is a life-threatening event. Yet there is freedom in that. I love how Kavin Rowe puts it, "When we accept the truth about our mortality, we can also experience remarkable freedom: to take the time to say 'I love you'…to examine our beliefs about what really, really counts in life… even to pray."[10]

---

10 C. Kavin Rowe. "Dying Gives Us a Chance to Confront Truth." Wall Street Journal April 23, 2020; https://www.wsj.com/articles/dying-gives-us-a-chance-to-confront-truth-11587682436.

So many of our relationships in life can be strained at times. Especially with one's parents. Yet perhaps this Covid time can be one when we reflect on what is most important in life, and to look with grace upon our parents. Perhaps we can even express that now.

Parenting as a Spiritual Practice

It is often said that "It takes a village to raise a child." Parenting is not just an activity for a child's parents, but for their grandparents, aunts and uncles, older siblings, and teachers who play a role. A church community is like a village in that way as well. Each one of us not only was or is a child but touches the life of some young person in ways we may not realize.

Nancy Fuchs-Kreimer's excellent book, *The Spirituality of Parenting*, suggests that while we pass religion down to our children, spirituality is often passed upwards.[11] Some people find their most spiritual selves in parenting. One of the parents in Bible Music Camp at our church has described to me how their experience of parenting is a profoundly spiritual practice. A privilege. A sacred calling. A way to touch the future.

After our first child was born my wife and I were overwhelmed. Our early days were a blur. We were exhausted. We tried for days to get our baby to sleep. We took turns taking him around the block in the stroller hoping he'd fall asleep. Those were tough days. Yet we also marveled at the miracle of life in our midst. At the opportunity and blessing we had of being able to raise him and shape his life. And all our kids.

Think about how much your children or grandchildren or children somewhere in your experience have taught you

---

11 Nancy Fuchs-Kreimer. *The Spirituality of Parenting*. Jewish Lights Publisher, 1998.

about the most sacred principles of your faith. Consider the theological ideas of our faith and then ponder what you have learned about them from being a parent. What you learned about love. The feeling you had when you first laid eyes on your child. The unconditional love deep within you which you can't help but express. The love you had when you held your child close. That is the kind of unconditional love that God has for each of us.

Think about what you learned about creation. A child that grew inside you for nine months and then grows outside of you. Your children may be made in your image, but you all were made in the image of God. Some of you may be taking a child to college this year if the path is clear from Covid. You look at your child and realize how much they have grown.

The creation doesn't just start with you. Billy Graham once said that to him, "the birth of a baby was the greatest proof of the existence of God."

Being a parent teaches us about other parts of God's creation in nature. Kids make us think about creation around us. Have you ever wondered why is it that kids are so crazy about animals? My children are all fascinated with animals, from the itsy-bitsy spider to their obsession with our dog. On the way back from our trip to Cape Cod once our family stopped at the Mystic Aquarium in Connecticut. It was worth it to see the whales swim around the pool right before your eyes. A perfect place for a fieldtrip. Then on the car ride home the next day we played a video called "Really Wild Animals" over and over and over again, but as a result I learned about some really wild animals in God's creation.

What have your children taught you about forgiveness? I watch our twins compete and push and cry. But then they reconcile and support.

Do those of you who are parents experience the witching hour? That time around dinner when the kids are just most rowdy and running around. When our two boys are being rowdy, it takes everything in my power not to get upset. I often employ the holy trinity of parenting, "Don't make me count to 3." But you learn from those situations. I learn about grace. We tell our children to say, "I'm sorry," and find ourselves internalizing our own words about grace. For in grace is how God acts towards us. God forgives us through Jesus Christ. Think about how often you have to forgive something a child does? Then realize how many things we all did as children that needed to be forgiven. Then ponder what we all still do as adults that we need forgiveness for. Fortunately, God forgives us our sins, as we forgive those who sin against us.

What have your children taught you about humility? Children force us to slow down, to listen and focus on the present. My mother used to talk about how hard it was to get out of the house with me as a child. She would get me changed and all ready to go and then I would spill something, and she'd never get out of the house. Now I am experiencing the same thing as a parent. It takes forever to get out of house.

Yet there is something healthy in taking our time. In slowing down. Of finding the spiritual in the mundane. We are forced to do that within this Covid time. Children have to learn things we take for granted. There is something healthy about learning about humility.

What has parenting taught you about your own beliefs? Being a parent may bring you face to face with your ideals as you try and explain them to your children.

I once spent a night at a camp for those without a home behind White Flint Mall in our Montgomery County, Maryland, with case workers from Bethesda Cares. We returned and talked with our kids about the need for justice.

My younger son said we should give the people who lived in the camp a home. I couldn't answer why we didn't.

One of the ideals for many of us is the importance of going to church. Many of us who weren't active in a church as young adults return to church as parents for our children. Just being in the church community matters for children. Just being in church, hearing its rhythm, is instructive. I used to sit in the balcony of my church in Ohio for years as a child and I didn't think I was paying attention. As an adult, as a pastor, I can look back and I realize how much I did pick up.

Children make us act on our beliefs as they help us remember to be on our best behavior. We want to model good behavior for them. Kids learn by example. They watch us, what we communicate by the way we speak, by the way we treat others, and by the decisions we make. This is how children learn. So, we start to say prayers at dinner that we might not otherwise say except we feel we should around them. The Book of Proverbs tells us "Train children in the right way and when old, they will not stray."

Parenting gets many of us thinking about the future. About mortality. About taking care of ourselves. I understand in some countries there is a custom of making the cross on a child's head whenever a parent leaves them. That is sign I have made many evenings on my children at bedtime as I say the "Now I lay me down to sleep; I give thee Lord my soul to keep. If I should die before I wake, I give thee Lord my soul to take."[12]

Children make us think about our own mortality. That we might not be here forever and that our children will continue after we are gone. When we say goodnight to kids,

---

[12] Famous 18th century prayer.

many times we read a story. We hope the story of our lives continues with our children.

We drove back from a vacation once and out of the blue one of our boys asked, "Dad, will Batman go to Heaven?" You have to think about these subjects for yourself as you explain it to them.

One evening recently one of our children asked about death. We asked if he knew what death was. He said that "Death is when you fall down. And you stay down for a really really really long time. And then you get up and go to Heaven to be with God." That is great Pauline theology. I got a lump in my throat as I heard him share it. It was very spiritual moment.

Whenever my mother visited early on, she brought clothes that belonged to my sister to try on our 18-month-old twins. But eventually our children grow up. We can't dress them as we like any longer. They become independent. And we need that. I have heard it said that from age birth to 5 a child needs someone to care for them. From 6-12 someone to teach them things. From ages 12-20 a coach. From 21 on, a friend. Parenting in every stage is a calling. A sacred calling.

Jesus took children seriously. He loved them and called them to himself. He referred to God as his heavenly father, underscoring the importance of the parenting role. Jesus preached about the importance of self-sacrifice.

Is there a better mantra for being a parent than "it's not about you?" When you are a parent you learn that pretty fast. If anything will help you see it's not about you, its parenting. That is a profoundly spiritual idea.

In the end, having children should make us laugh. That is a good spiritual practice. That is good for the soul. We have to laugh sometimes at the challenges and the absurd parts of life. The crazy things that happen when kids say and do amazing things. I don't know how many times my wife and I have looked at each other and said, "We need to write that down." Kids give parents permission to laugh at themselves and that is good for the soul.

We are a village that will raise the next generation. Every one of us has a role to play in nurturing someone. Young people will teach you things of the spirit. They will remind you that you are a child of God.

We all were children once. We are all children of God now.

How can this Covid moment make you appreciate your parents? Write down your thoughts to them in a letter.

Paul and Philippi

The Apostle Paul's letter to the church at Philippi is one of his most heartfelt letters. It was one of what are called his prison letters, which Paul wrote from a cell in Rome or Ephesus. It shows us a lot about Paul the person. It teaches us how we might relate to those entities which maybe support us, those we can have differing, and sometimes difficult, relationships with. For parents often support us financially at times. Not always, but often parents invest a lot in a child. I have read that according to the U.S. Department of Agriculture in 2017, the average cost of raising a baby born in 2015 from birth through age 17 is $233,610.[13]

In Philippians 1, Paul writes of his close collaboration with the Philippian church. He writes that they had been together through thick and thin, partnering in ministry, and were always in his heart. Paul had walked many journeys with the Philippians. Paul was at some level financially dependent

---

13 https://www.usda.gov/media/blog/2017/01/13/cost-raising-child.

upon churches like the one in Philippi. He was grateful for their gift of financial support.

Paul's writes a somewhat complex statement of acknowledgement to a church which had given him support. We can tell Paul has mixed feelings about it. He was perhaps a little guilty for accepting the gift. Paul writes a kind of thank you note, yet never says thank you. Paul jokes that it took them long enough to get him aid saying "at last" they sent it, suggests he doesn't really seek or even need their support. He acts a bit passive aggressively towards those who have just sent him financial aid. We can too towards parents. Paul attempts to assert his independence from the Philippians and freedom from reliance on material things, saying that he has gotten to a point of contentment whether or not he received their financial support.

The relationship Paul describes with the Philippians is like that of a child with a parent. Children and parents walk many journeys together. Children are often dependent on parents financially. Children are often grateful to their parents for love and lessons and support. Because children eventually leave the nest, they, at some point, become like Paul and begin to assert independence.

There are many of us where our relationships with our parents now are vital and meaningful and cherished. There are many who miss their parents and treasure their lessons. There are others here for whom thoughts about their parents are full of pain. For many of us, the relationship with one or both of our parents are complicated.

Perhaps a Covid spiritual practice for us could be writing a letter to our parents.

All of us have a relationship with some parental figure, whether our biological parents or adoptive parents. Whether a grandparent or teacher or mentor or coach.

Writing a letter to them can be a healthy spiritual act for you and perhaps for them.

Before Paul's letter to Philippi, the town, named for Alexander the Great's father, was largely known for a great battle. In the year 63bc, a child, Octavian was born in Rome and grew up in the royal court. In the year 45bc, Julius Caesar declared the first leap year. The following year, Caesar was famously killed by Cassius and Brutus. Not because of leap year, but over political differences.

Octavian had been adopted as Julius Caesar's son and heir and became emperor. He was furious about what happened to his father and went to avenge his father's death.

So, the following year, at a town called Philippi in northern Greece, one of the great battles in ancient history took place. Octavian and Mark Antony and their armies fought Cassius and Brutus and their armies. The battle of Philippi was critical to lifting up Octavian and his consolidating power and led to a renewed Roman empire. When Octavian eventually became the ruler of a stronger Roman Empire, he took the name Caesar Augustus. Yes, that Caesar Augustus.

Eventually, as Luke's Gospel tells us in a famous statement, "In those days a decree went out from Emperor Caesar Augustus that all the world should be part of a census."

It was during this very registration that a man named Joseph took his wife, Mary, to Bethlehem, where their child was born. If Octavian had not been motivated by his father's death to fight at battle at Philippi, Mary might not have given birth to Jesus in Bethlehem.

Jesus grew up and modeled true connection, equality, and love with his heavenly parent through the trinity.

There can be differing feelings towards parents at different times. Those who support us physically, financially, and emotionally, are important and deserve to be honored. The fifth of the ten commandments is to "honor your father and mother." This revelation to Moses helps us know the importance of respecting and expressing our gratitude towards our parents. It is interesting to note that the word "honor" is a broad one in Hebrew, meaning not just one act, but a general attitude. The context of this command applied to adults, as well as or even more so than children.

There is often great wisdom we gain from our parents and grandparents whether we realize it or not. Mark Twain famously said, "When I was a boy of 14, my father was so ignorant I could hardly stand it. But by the time I was 21, I was astonished at how much the old man had learned in seven years."

There is wisdom that comes with age and experience. One friend asked me recently if I thought Jesus made mistakes. Jesus didn't sin, he was fully God, but he was also fully human and learned from trial and error. Luke 2: 52 reveals that even Jesus "grew in wisdom," as he grew up. He grew in wisdom from experience. We all learn from experience. Our parents and grandparents have wide experience as well.

Jack Welch died in 2020. Welch was the CEO of General Electric (GE) and was hailed as one of the most successful CEO's in America. GE was the most valuable company in the world under Welch and Fortune Magazine called him the manager of the century. Welch was once asked the secret of his success and he answered, his mother. He called his mother, Grace, the most influential person in his life, who taught him to get the best out of people. We all have memories of parents. Writing can help us come to terms with them.

Writing to Our Parents

For some of us, there will be a time when the window will close on writing a letter that our parents can appreciate. Family dynamics can be complicated and for some it can be easier to write our feelings in a letter than to express them out loud. For others of us, whose parents have passed, there may be something we have been holding inside that we never said in person but writing out those thoughts can be healthy. I spend more time in cemeteries than the average person perhaps and I can't tell you how many letters I have seen leaning up against tombstones.

Whether it's a word of gratitude or an expression of frustration. Whether a heartfelt thought of compassion or an assertion of independence. Whatever it is, writing a letter to our parents can be part of our personal expression. It can mean a lot to a parent who receives it. It can create a breakthrough in dialogue when we can't find the words in person. It can help us release and free emotions we have been carrying with us for a long time so that we can be freed.

Jesus said, "Unless you become like little children, you will never enter the kingdom of God." John tells us, "To all who those received him and believed in his name, he gave the power to become children of God." Being dependent on God allows for the freedom, independence, and strength to face the emotions and express what it is we need to express. Writing such a letter can be a special social distancing spiritual practice.

For some of us, our relationship with our parents is a source of fear. We fear a memory from the past. We fear we don't live up to expectations. We fear what life will be like without our parents here. There is no shortage of television characters, both fathers and mothers, who are intimidating, even abusive, frightening, or scary. Thinking about our parents can be challenging for many of us.

Writing a letter to our parents, for some, can bring freedom. Freedom from the memory that binds us or from the pain that traps us.

Freedom is a theme of part of Paul's letter to the Philippians. Paul was asserting a kind of independence in his letter to Philippi, that he was not dependent on things, that he could get by in plenty and in want, because of God. Not self-sufficient, but what some commentators call "God-sufficient." Paul famously writes, "I can do all things through him who strengthens me." Paul was saying he is not defined by his possessions or his lack of them, but by a relationship with God which allows him to go beyond them. He could do all things through God who strengthens him.

For some of us, it can help to involve God in prayer when we take the step of writing to our parents.

There can be real benefit in getting things off our chest, in facing our pain and fears, and in writing a letter to them.

Or for some of us, to say a word of thanks while we still can.

Even if we don't have a relationship with a parent or if our parents are no longer living, there can be value in writing a letter to them as if they were still alive. To connect through the spirit with parents. To be able to say something we didn't or couldn't in life. Or to do the same to a teacher or mentor.

Not long ago, I was back in Ohio with a family member of my parents' generation whose health is faltering. This person has suffered from severe pain her whole life and complications made for a very painful and difficult time. As she and I talked about some tough choices she had to make, I was struck by her calm faith in the future. As I drove her to dialysis, we talked about some of the things she had to give up. She was in a prolonged state of fasting. But in her wilderness, she developed a new relationship with God that allowed her to face great fears with grace and strength. What impressed me most was that she was able to live with hope for the future that inspired me. As I left, I wrote a note to this person, who was a caregiver, a teacher, like a parent to me.

Use this Covid-retreat to write a note to a parent figure.

This year, 2020, my parents moved from the house they had lived in since 1975 to a smaller place. I flew to Ohio on March 8, right as the pandemic hit, to help them weed things out as they downsize. As many of you know, letting things go after decades of careful preservation and care is not easy. I was preparing to need to support my parents in their emotions of this transition and to pay attention to my own emotions of letting go of the house where I grew up.

There was a tinge of sadness already in saying goodbye to my childhood home. A sense of vulnerability, of being uprooted, of facing my own inevitable mortality in it all, combined with the resignation that this is necessary, and excitement of some new freedom for my parents of not having to care for a house which isn't set up well for their future needs. Yet I look forward with hope to what the future brings. For with God we can do all things through God who strengths us.

I got off the plane last March and saw my parents as I prepared to go back to our childhood home for what was the last time. It brought up thoughts and feelings for me and my parents. One of the first things I did when I got off the plane was hand them two handwritten letters. I'd written to them, in my best handwriting, on stationary my mom had bought me many years ago, using one of the left-handed-smear proof pens she gave me. To say thank you and more.

Prayer

Loving God, help us honor our mother and father, to seek with gratitude and honesty those who have gone before us, and to find you, our heavenly parent, in our reflections. Amen.

Chapter Five
A Letter to a Significant Person

Combating Isolation

This Covid-retreat is a crisis where so many are isolated. There are major disruptions in life. We need to do our social distancing and create isolation for our health. However, social isolation, especially for our seniors, is already a major health issue. We know from various media reports that the mental health impacts of social isolation on the elderly, on children, and on all, is growing as a result from the virus situation.

For many of our senior volunteers at the church, being engaged is a lifeline. Yet social distancing is encouraging us to put our "being active" with other human beings on hold.

I was planning to lead worship at a local nursing home the very weekend the virus hit in force here and all shut down, but that was cancelled as many assisted living and senior centers were restricting outside visitors, and will be for a long time.

This crisis does not define us, however. The congregation I currently serve was very involved with HIV/AIDS crisis years ago. They held concerts to raise funds and try and deal with the challenges of that time. I put up a banner from one of our HIV/AIDS concerts from our past on our chancel because the congregation had been on the forefront of helping those in need due to a health crisis before. This was to remind us that crises involving a virus have not prevented God from being present and worshipped in our space before.

The day I put the banner up, I shared that I read, not from the book of Covid, chapter 19, but from Paul's letter to the Romans chapter 1. And it's better news.

St. Paul's letter to the Romans is considered by many to be Paul's greatest letter. Written around 58 a.d., most likely from Corinth, it is a unique letter. Most of Paul's letters were written to churches he had founded or communities he had spent time with. Most addressed specific problems that had arisen in those communities. Many addressed disputes between specific people or looked to challenges that had arisen in the life of the particular church community.

Yet Paul had never visited Rome when he wrote this letter. He didn't know the people directly. He wasn't aware of their individual or intimate challenges. Paul writes a more formal and less personal letter than he usually does here. He chooses his words carefully. He writes more pages to the Romans than to any other church. He introduces himself to a community who didn't know him.

In many ways it is a letter about Paul's individual theology. Some say preaching is a dialogue where the meaning of the theology, the text, the word of God, and the meaning of the context of a congregation, meet. Well, Paul didn't have as much of a context for this Roman congregation at this point. So, we get more of Paul's theology in this letter. His letter to the Romans is perhaps his most complete theological treatise as a result.

Paul writes that he announces the Gospel of Jesus. Gospel means good news. We have had a lot of bad news in our world in the last few months. We need good news.

Paul writes that he is not ashamed. We should not be ashamed when things aren't perfect. That is sometimes ok.

Paul writes that we no longer need to live lives that are afraid. We no longer need to live in fear. We no longer need to fear for God holds us. The good news is we don't need to be afraid because God can reach us anywhere. No matter what we are facing, God can be with us.

What Faith Gives

Paul famously writes in his letter to the Roman church that "the righteous live by faith." He includes that idea in other letters too.

That phrase is a reference to the 7th century Old Testament prophet Habakkuk. Habakkuk was concerned about injustice in society in greater Israel and Judah.

When Paul writes about righteousness here, he does not mean perfect action or ideal ethics, he means a right relationship with God. For God seeks to walk alongside us. We need that now.

Paul's letter suggests we walk by faith. We walk by faith not by fear. Faith gives confidence. Confidence that God walks with us and holds us in the palm of God's hand, even during such times as this Covid crisis.

In a time when we wonder where to turn, we can turn to God. Faith gives hope. We trust, depend on, and rely on God.

Faith gives salvation. We are saved ultimately by God. We are also saved by our being responsible. The virus' impact on us in some ways is up to us. We can help to slow its spread through our behavior. We need to be responsible as a nation.

Faith gives power. We are not stuck with nothing to do during this time. We can do something, even in our seeming isolation. This is an inward focused season of making the best of our solitude.

Yet, this can be an outward focused time in a way too.

For faith gives action.

This has been a season of anger for many of us. There are racial tensions and protests and rallies and challenges. We are stunned by the horrific killing of an unarmed black man, George Floyd. Feeling shocked, saddened, and frustrated at the continued injustices, inequities, and divisions in our nation, along with the misguided response from some, all with the backdrop of the U.S. surpassing well over 100,000 deaths from the virus.

In the book of Genesis, we read that God brings humans to life by giving us breath to our lungs. When George Floyd was brutally held down and choked to death in May 2020, he cried, "I can't breathe." As it was been asked, "what could be further from God's hope for creation?"

We think about breath from Covid, a lack of breath for many people who are on venerators. The healthy among us wear masks, but many cannot breathe well in them.

When Jesus died, Matthew 27 tells us he took his last breath. He died by crucifixion, which was an ancient way of depriving someone of oxygen.

The word for spirit and breath in Hebrew, *ruach*, is the same. Jesus went to heaven, but the Holy Spirit arrived.

In the New Testament, at Pentecost, we celebrate the giving of the Holy Spirit. The breath of God for God's people. Our nation continues to protest and rally and think of change in the wake of George Floyd's death.

One June morning in 2020, our family went down to Lafayette Square, the park around the White House in downtown D.C., to show our kids the protest site, St. John's church and the barrier around the park, and to pay respects. On the barrier around the White House were many artistic and colorful signs. My attention was caught by a man with an unusual boom box playing loud music and wearing a T-Shirt with a saying from 2 Corinthians on it about reconciliation with God. As I watched him dance, over his shoulder on the wall was a series of crosses. In the middle of them was a sign which read, "The future called, and it needs more action now."

As we think about the activities we plan to do as a world in standing up for what is right, we do so with Christ around us. We do so for the sake of change. For the sake of God's love.

That change is possible for a nation. That gives hope for the future for us as we look to think about making a more perfect union.

We must be open to hearing the pain of others. To have the sustained commitment and unity for this time and beyond. For the sake of the future. Our country's and our own.

Writing from a Distance

Paul writes to the Romans that he was unable to visit them. He says he wanted to visit them but was prevented. Paul makes that point clear that he was prevented from physically being with the people he wanted to be with.

That is how many of us feel now with the virus.

Paul couldn't go exactly where he wanted to. Paul experienced in his own way some social distancing.

So, what did he do about it when he couldn't visit the Romans in person? He wrote them a letter.

During this period of social distancing, let me suggest we write a letter, a brief, handwritten note, and mail it to someone, beginning with seniors, one each day, or one a week, for as long our social distancing lasts. This is a way for folks to stay connected to their church family. As one friend put it, "perhaps receiving something other than a bill or solicitation would be welcome."

Or, rather than mailing a letter, I am thinking the personal touch of calling and hearing another warm voice is another option. So, we could call at least one other member of your church or social circle or family, one a day or week, a regular schedule, starting with your senior members, during this time of social distancing. Let's create our own calling tree where we reach out and look out for each other.

If you are feeling isolated at this time, perhaps writing a note, or calling a church member or friend can be a healthy way to stay connected with your faith community and friends as you visualize your community here. Be a community of caring.

This is what Paul did in a way. Writing a letter to the church at Rome was unique as this was a community at a distance. The distance was overcome by his honest, heartfelt letter. Along with phone calls, perhaps it can be for us too.

These are anxious and uncertain times. Yet we have faith in a strong, sovereign, and loving God. We will get through this together by God's grace. Pray for strength, healing, wisdom, and peace for all. We will come back together when the time is right. No challenge can change Christ's victory over death. Paul knew that nothing in life or the life to come can separate us from the love of God.

Letter to a Spouse

Paul's letter to the Thessalonians is the first Christian letter, the first words of Christian literature. 1 Thessalonians is the first New Testament book written; the earliest book written in the New Testament. If Paul's letters were in chronological order, First Thessalonians would be before Romans. If the New Testament were in chronological order, 1 Thessalonians, not Matthew, would be its first book. Paul wrote this letter in around 51 a.d. to a church in Greece called Thessalonica.

In it, Paul describes how he went to Thessalonica, the capital of the providence of Macedonia with his friends, Silas, and Timothy, and started a church there. It was hard starting the church there. Acts and 1 Thessalonians tell us how there was great opposition and even violence from what are called "ruffians" who didn't like his preaching. This is the one upside to my preaching to an empty room, I guess, these days – no potential for an angry mob. Paul and the others were lucky to get out with their lives. They made it to southern Greece, to Athens and Corinth.

They were separated from the Thessalonians, so sent Timothy to check on them and he reported that they were doing well. So, from Corinth, Paul wrote a letter to the Thessalonians praising them for all the good they were doing and faith they had.

Paul begins his letter to the Thessalonians by connecting faith and work. This is something Paul often did. In his letter to the Philippians, for example, Paul writes famously that we should work out our salvation with fear and trembling. By connecting faith to work he was saying let our faith inspire us to do something. He adds work to faith to encourage Thessalonians. To do something with their faith.

Love requires work. Many of us have found that in this time as our schedules change, and we are cooped up on our homes with people we love but aren't used to being with all the time.

We are in our houses in close quarters with our family and our relationships needs support. There is the phrase about couples being married "for better for worse, but not for lunch."

So be extra kind to your family now. Love is labor when we all confined together. Perhaps it's right to write to our significant others. Write to your spouse or partner.

My own context now is our have four school age kids under 13 in our home with our puppy and our house is under construction, so we've had no kitchen since the fall. Plus, my mother in law is with us quarantined, and my wife and I are trying to work from home and stay connected but are trying to find activities for the kids.

Take a moment in some way to communicate to your significant others at home what you are feeling.

Many men grew facial hair during this time. That wasn't always popular at my home when I did so.

I will never forget years ago, the first month of my first call as a full-time pastor. A phone call late at night to come to the nursing home. The news that someone beloved would not make it. Coming into the room, a large room with a small bed. In bright lights inside and darkness outside, giving a final prayer. In that moment, a dear friend kissing his wife on the forehead and saying, "I'll see you up there, love." Nothing can separate us from the love of God.

Do I believe we will see our loved ones again? I do. Because of the power of love. Death does not defeat that power. And it won't keep us apart either.

Many of us when we think about significant others, think of spouses. Many of us wrote love letters once, but email has replaced letter writing. Perhaps this is a time to write a letter again to a spouse or significant other.

For others of us, we miss our life partner. Some will lose someone during this Covid time. We wonder if we will see our life partners again.

We are all worried about this virus, and it makes us think about death.

The Bible does not have a whole lot to say about what happens to us when we die. However, the witness of scripture is that death is not the end. That God will welcome us home.

We each love people in this life. At their death, we grieve. We hurt. We are in pain. Grief fades, but many scars never go away.

This is because humans are made for relationship. We are not made to easily detach from each other. We are made to love.

So, we continue to love people even after they die. It is important to reflect on the fact that love does not end with death.

If our scriptures tell us anything it is that God is love. John makes that point over and over. God is love.

If God is love, and love doesn't end with death, then God's relationship with us won't either.

When Paul wrote to the Romans about God's faithful, lasting, loving relationship with us, he wrote as someone for whom God could have turned God's back. Paul used to put Christians to death. Yet, God loved him still. If God would not let Paul go, God will not let us go either.

Love is about relationships. Heaven is about relationships too. If you think about the Bible, the Gospels tell us that Jesus did not die alone. Two criminals were crucified with him, one on either side. Jesus said, "today you will be with me in paradise."

Nothing separates us from the love of God.

A few months ago, I sat with a man who had lived a full life. He made great contributions to his church. He loved his children. He had a successful career. Above all he loved his wife. He bought flowers for her even until late in their lives, until the week she died. At the end, I could talk with him about death. He was ready to die. He looked forward. He said he looked forward to seeing her at the end.

All of us have someone who's hoped-for presence makes the other side of death a little easier to take. Whether it's a spouse, a child, a sibling, a friend, or whether it's Jesus. The one who goes before us, who prepares a dwelling place for you and for me.

I can recall standing around a hospital bed not too long ago. The heart attack was taking the body, as well as breaking the heart of the family who was faced with difficult choices. When the machines were turned off, he breathed his last. We gathered on either side of the bed, held hands, and prayed. We knew that nothing separates us from the love of God.

I remember a friend saying not too long ago of a child, "I love her too much to let death remove her from us." All we could share in that moment is what we hold onto during this virus crisis, that God will not let death take us away from the love of God either.

Through God's love in Jesus, death has lost its ultimate power over us. We are not lost — because nothing separates us from the love of God.

I think of relatives in my own family. They met later in life. They treasured each other and their time together. One took care of the other at the end. Their grief remained strong. Yet so does their love. Death has not ended it. God's love is bigger than anything we can do to separate ourselves from God.

Why would an infinite being make us if something we do for a short time on earth ruins our being with that infinite God forever? Love wins. For our personal destiny is wrapped up in what we believe about Jesus' destiny. Jesus makes a path for us to walk to God in eternity. Nothing separates us from God's love.

God has not revealed much of what Heaven looks like in scripture. Maybe the great joy and meaning of it is a surprise and it's good that we will be able to celebrate more when we get there because we don't know exactly what was coming. The purpose of the Bible is not to tell us exactly what happens next in Heaven. Its purpose includes telling us how to live in the meantime in response. The answer is to live with confidence that we will be with God and to live in love.

Our faith teaches that we need not be afraid of death. Because nothing will separate us from God's love.

As we watched many doctors and nurses in New York and elsewhere bravely deal with this virus crisis, and put themselves on the front lives, we think about significant people we admire. There have been many heroes during this time. Maybe we should recognize them through our letters, a letter of thanks to front line workers.

Letter to a Mentor

There are many of us for whom a mentor, particularly a teacher, has shaped our life. Someone who was not a parent, but who was like a parent figure to us.

Perhaps write a letter to them. Write to a teacher or mentor.

We are now living into a time of solitude. Paul wrote, "you do not need to have anyone write to you…we urge you… to live quietly, to mind your own affairs…"

Living quietly is what many of us are doing. We are living in solitude. We don't need letters perhaps, but they might help.

There are upsides of quarantine. One friend sent me a list of positive things about the quarantine. Pollution reduction. Very light traffic. Relief from our frenzied schedules. Learning to adjust to calm.

How will you make use of this quiet time? This solitude.

Who are the heroes in your life? Parents can be. A teacher or mentor can be. A dear mentor of mine died last June. I had the privilege of giving a prayer right before his memorial service this past fall. Think of all our significant people in life.

Jesus invites us to put our trust and our lives in his hands. Into his outstretched hands.

God's love is a gift. God came into our messy, imperfect world to be in eternal relationship with us and to give us hope for loving reunion. Nothing in life or death will change that.

Letter to a Peer

There was a tree in our front yard at home in Ohio growing up, a big magnolia tree, that I used to love to climb as a boy. It had strong branches and big pink leaves. For the first few years we lived in that house my friends would come over and we'd have lots of fun climbing that tree. As we grew, it served as home base for our kickball and baseball games. Later it was a place for me to sit among fragrant leaves and share thoughts with good friends. That tree and its branches became a symbol of friendship for me.

Jesus was interested in friendship. He talked about it in the New Testament. He was also interested in his disciples' spiritual and personal growth. Jesus didn't just want them to be blind lemmings, he wanted them to develop their own spiritual core, for he knew they would need to continue God's work after his death. I find it encouraging that Jesus was interested in the growth of those who would follow him. The key for the disciples, as the branches of God, was to remain rooted in the vine that was their Lord even as they grew. Especially as they grew.

For many of us, Facebook is aa critical communications tool. The key to Facebook is the act of "friending" people. You can tell people what you are doing in real time, but first, in order to link to people as "friends," one has to send a "friend request," which the other person has to accept. I know people who have gotten very competitive about the number of Facebook "friends" they have, compiling long lists of hundreds of "friends."

Having lots of friends is a nice thing. But perhaps we only need a few good friends. My grandmother would say, "If you have one true friend you are lucky." Jesus sent out his disciples "two by two" to do their work in the world. Jesus didn't send them out by the hundreds, but in pairs.

Our faith can teach us something about friendship. Jesus shook up his culture through relationships of love, not power and intimidation. He didn't come bullying as many political, military and even religious authorities of the day did, but he made friends by being a friend.

Jesus said that there is no greater love than laying down life for one's friends. During this Covid time, an Italian priest, Don Giuseppe Berardelli, gave up his ventilator, which his parish members had bought for him, to save a younger patient. There is no greater love than such sacrifice.

My closest friend from junior high is still a very close friend, one I rely on emotionally. Growing up he would give the largest half of the cookie to me and later would be quick to pay for dinner when we were out in later years. When I needed him at most crucial times, he was always there.

Maybe you have a close friend to whom you might write.

One of my favorite moments from the Academy Awards show in 2010 was when actor Tim Robbins introduced Morgan Freedman in the segment where Freeman was being nominated for the best actor award by saying,

"Morgan and I became friends working together on the movie *The Shawshank Redemption*.[14] The film follows a friendship and that friendship was easily mirrored on the set by us." Tim Robbins said, "I'll never forget what Morgan said to me about friendship on the last day of shooting. He said, 'Being a friend is getting the other a cup of coffee. Can you do that for me Ted? It is Ted, isn't it?'" A funny moment. Real friendship can't be all about you.

What do we make of Jesus' statement in John 15 when he says, "I do not any longer call you servants, but I call you friends." If friends are our equals, here Jesus is talking to his disciples who are certainly not his equals. Well, in sharing everything with them, telling the disciples everything they needed to know and not holding back, Jesus was lowering himself and raising them up so that they might abide in each other. That they might have a mutual relationship like a tree or a vine and its branches. One cannot tell easily where the vines and branches begin and end. They are all part of the same plant. Jesus is the vine and the branches cannot produce fruit unless they abide in the vine. Jesus is searching for mutuality in relationships, not hierarchy. That is friendship. We are all in this imperfect life together and do well to abide in each other.

We cannot manufacture friendship on our own. It takes two. But we can open ourselves to friendship. Be open to being a friend, to being nice to people we've met, to being hospitable. Caring for another, taking time for the other, listening to others, being attentive to the wants and needs of others.

Friends keep us strong. They remind us that we are not alone. That we face the challenge of life together. As the

---

14 *The Shawshank Redemption*. Directed by Frank Darabont, Castle Rock Entertainment, 1994. Film.

branches of God, we do well to stay rooted in the vine that is Jesus Christ and to remember what Christ teaches.

Friendships can make life more tolerable and wonderful.

Let us write to our friends, our peers, our buddies, and tell them what they mean to us. What they mean to you.

I love how Paul writes to the Thessalonians, "When we were made orphans by being separated from you—in person, not in heart—we longed with great eagerness to see you face to face." Many of us are separated from work and friends and church, in person, but not in heart. We long to see and be seen face to face. What a great phrase.

Write or reach out to a friend. Write to someone who is isolated, or to your spouse or partner or to a mentor or to a friend. Write to them and tell that you care.

Prayer

Loving God, be with us and help us form deep relationships with others. That they may mirror your love for us. For the sake of your son we pray. Amen.

Chapter Six
A Letter to a Future Generation

Writing to Our Children

Our children can bring us some of our greatest concerns, but also some of our most joyful moments in life. One of our daughters likes to run around the house singing, "Time spent with Daddy is time well spent." I love that. It makes me think about investing time in what we do for those who follow us. For many of us, our children mean the world to us. For all of us, we care about what we leave behind to, for and through someone, our children or someone in the world.

We think about those who will go after us. For us during this time, we care for the world and what it will become.

The virus tests us. It makes us confront our mortality. To picture a world in which we are not present in it. We are called not to give up on this world. This was early problem in Thessalonica. Some were giving up on this world. Paul writes one part of 2 Thessalonians to tell people to not just look at the sky, but to look for what is in front of them. The early Christians in Thessalonica expected the second coming of Jesus to happen very soon, and that was making them idle.

Paul wrote about "idleness" and suggested the people should not sit idle or give up. They should not just be idle believing the world was about to end. Instead, they were to get with it.

This is a hard time. Yet don't give up on this world. Don't give up. For young people, who will inherit the world, care about it. They want to be involved in the world. Write to them about the importance of being involved. They will respond.

How do we do that, how to we stay engaged when we are supposed to stay socially distant?

One of friend wrote to me, "Every fiber of my being tells me that I should be out doing something to help other people address this crisis, but every doctor I have tells me 'don't you dare.'" How do we offer home-bound support for the world?

One option is to write a note to the generations that will follow you.

I have a good friend from my church who regularly puts a note in the niche in our columbarium, near to where her son lies. That is meaningful to her. She sometimes puts a note in the niche to communicate to him. He has gone before her in death, but she can still feel his presence.

Paul wrote to the Thessalonians, "Therefore encourage one another and build up each other, as indeed you are doing." That includes encouraging our children.

As a friend wrote to me, this remains a surreal time. When I wake up in the morning I keep wondering, "Was this all a dream?"

Then I look at the news and see something happened and it was worse than what happened yesterday, and I know it's not a dream.

This is a time when the world needs us to be public minded. Ironically, staying home is being public minded. Wearing a mask is caring about the future.

Use this as a time to teach the next generation about Sabbath. That is one issue that is particularly challenging and in some ways a luxury, as many families with kids and workers don't have flexibility or an ability to take time off.

How does this time change us? How do we react to it? Does it bring out bad behavior? Or can we become more gracious towards and tolerant of others?

In this time can we teach our children to be more humble? To see in ourselves what we recognize in others.

Paul encouraged the Thessalonians and all churches to do something with their faith, and we are called as well, as the "twin viruses" of Covid and racism meant that 2020 is a time of great pain for so many.

Paul wrote two letters to a man named Timothy. Timothy followed Paul on his trips and was his mentee. Paul wrote near the beginning of his first letter, "To Timothy, my beloved child…I am grateful to God—whom I worship with a clear conscience, as my ancestors did—when I remember you constantly in my prayers night and day. Recalling your tears, I long to see you so that I may be filled with joy. I am reminded of your sincere faith, a faith that lived first in your grandmother Lois and your mother Eunice and now, I am sure, lives in you. For this reason, I remind you to rekindle the gift of God that is within you through the laying on of my hands; for God did not give us a spirit of cowardice, but rather a spirit of power and of love and of self-discipline."

This passage seems so much like a parent writing to a child. Paul says, "my beloved child." Parents are often grateful for and think of their children as beloved. They remember them in prayers. They miss them and long to see them so to be filled with joy.

Paul refers to Timothy's grandparents, as parents are often referring to their own parents, whose spirit now lives in them.

Finally, Paul reminds Timothy that God has given gifts for love and self-discipline. It sounds much like a parent's comments to a new graduate.

I have a good friend who traveled for several years out of the country for work. He'd leave each Sunday night to fly to Canada and would return the following Thursday. Each Sunday night he would write short notes and place them by his daughters' doors to tell them how much he loved them and missed them when he was gone.

This might be a time for us to write letters to the next generation.

To tell them what is on our hearts. To tell them of our faith. To let them know God in Christ loves them.

For so many young people, faith only becomes real when they see it enacted in the world. Write to our young people, yours, or others, and let them know they are needed to do the hard work of mission out in the world.

God's Grace for God's Children

As I mentioned, in what was his most personal letter, the Apostle Paul writes to his friend Timothy about how his mother, and those who went before, such as Eunice and Lois, helped instill in him the faith to become a follower of Christ.

It underscores the importance of mothers in our lives. How the example our mothers set for us and we as parents set for children help guide who we and they become. It is the grace of our mothers which helps reveal the heart of God.

Paul also refers to Timothy as "my beloved child," which is a helpful reminder that regardless of if we have been a physical parent or not, we can still experience the joy and privilege of being a mother or father figure in faith and life.[15] What is needed is grace.

In 1983, I went to Scotland for the first time with my mother. It was a trip through our church. I was just a bit older than our sons were when they went with me to Scotland for the first time.

When I asked my mother recently what she remembered about that trip, I thought she would wax eloquent about the heather on the hills or be nostalgic for the shortbread or about some castle. However, the memory that was most clear in her mind was that I wore a coat and tie every night for dinner. My mom recalls that our friend, Mr. Matheson on the trip, commented on nice I looked like a young lad dressed in my best. It was not how I probably had wanted to dress, but it made an impression on my mom.

What I remember most about the trip was the woman with the red umbrella. We had a petite, feisty, knowledgeable tour guide and her distinction was that she held up a red umbrella just over her head wherever we went, as a signal for us to go to her. It was her identity. It distinguished our group from other tour groups.

The tour guide held up the umbrella so we could identify her. So we didn't get lost. It was her calling card. That red umbrella was unique. It helped us know we belonged each time she placed it on top of her head.

Putting something on one's head has long been a symbol of identification. The Holy Spirit anointed heads in baptism in our tradition, and water does the same. The Psalmist famously wrote in Psalm 23 that the Lord anoints his head

---

15 William Barclay. *New Daily Study Bible*. "Timothy." Westminster John Knox Press. 2003. P. 160.

with oil. Israel's kings were anointed. Our new elders and deacons here are anointed.

Paul writes to Timothy that the gift of faith came when the leaders laid their hands on him. That was often done in ancient times by placing one's hands on a person's head.

In the Christian faith, it all starts with baptism. The sign of the cross with water on a child's head carries on the tradition of anointing.

The identification of a child with God at the start of life is an identification with grace. When we baptize a child we say, "Child of the covenant, I baptized you…" Child of the covenant means the covenant God began with God's people long before Christ which is culminated in the new covenant sealed in his blood which we celebrate when we pour the cup on a communion Sunday. That is the covenant of grace.

What is grace? Paul wrote of God's grace in several letters. St. Augustine, who has been called the "Professor of Grace," said, "It is only by God's grace that God has melted away the ice of my evil."

John Calvin believed faith was the certain knowledge of God's grace towards us.

Many scholars define grace as the "pure, unmerited favor of God."

To me, grace is God loving us completely as a mother would a child.

The Westminster Confession suggests, "In and for Jesus Christ, to make us partakers of the grace of adoption, we are taken into God's number to enjoy the liberties, privileges and responsibilities of the children of God… For all of us are the children of God, we are all God's offspring."

What exciting news. We are all children of God. Anointed and adopted. Once we realize that we are loved, accepted, forgiven, affirmed, cherished, it transforms who we are. That transformation is grace.

But we have to rediscover it every day. We have to accept the grace of God given to us in Jesus Christ.

We have to believe we are God's grace filled creations. That the liberties, privileges, and responsibilities of it are ours. The liberties are the freedom of a child under the protective wing of a mother. The responsibility of treating others as children of God.

When we give thanks for our parents, we affirm that caring for, nurturing, protecting, and growing, is a holy calling. Let us express that to our children.

My mother recently told me a robin had laid an egg outside her window. The mother robin left and hasn't come back. Each time my mother looks at that egg she feels a calling to put something on it to keep it warm. A prayer that the mother robin will come back.

We bring our concerns and thoughts to a God who loves each of us just as we are; that, we are children of God, anointed and adopted.

I remember a time on our trip to Scotland when my mom and I visited a family gravesite in the southeast of Scotland. On my mother's side the Scottish roots are in Duns southeast of Edinburgh and in borders area. I was tired, it was a long trip. I would walk a bit around the ground, but I was lonely. I was by far the youngest on the trip. I wasn't sure I belonged. I can remember standing in the rain beside gravesites from hundreds of years ago with the small group there and not really thinking I belonged. Then my mom took hold of my hand. She told me stories about family, which I wasn't really listening to. I just remember holding her hand. As the light broke into the dark Scottish sky, I felt that I connected, that I was part of something bigger than me, that I belonged.

Then soon after the women with the red umbrella reappeared. She brought me back to the tour again. As I held my mother's hand, I didn't soon forget that I belonged.

Let the next generation know they are God's children. Let someone who is different from you know they are God's children. May we all, whatever our circumstance, take hold of God's hand, discover we belong, and find our way to extend our hands.

Follow Christ in the Parade of Life

Last December, my daughters and I walked in the Alexandria Scottish parade. Decked out in kilts and gloves we tried to brave our way through a very cold parade with some other hearty folks. Until the wind whipped up and even our hearty 8-year-old suggested we stop. At the front of that parade was a man who held a mace. The Grand Marshal who led the parade. Often those famous parades on TV are led by what is called the Grand Marshall. A special person who is a focal point and who gets to lead the parade.

We are currently not allowed to have parades in our time. During this crisis, social distancing requires that we stay away from each other rather than gathering in groups for things like parades.

At church, we have a lot of the usual stuff in the worship services now as we livestream them. We have confessions and scripture and a sermon and beautiful music. We have online offerings and we have a children's moment and even communion. Most of what goes on a usual Sundays here we still have. Except we don't have the "parade," as one child called it. That is the moment at the beginning of the service when the call to worship ends and the choir director plays the organ music and the choir and pastors march up the front aisle into the choir loft and onto the chancel. This is our weekly parade.

We weep this year. This is a time when many of us are weeping. Much like Paul cried when he wrote to the Corinthians about the challenges there. Luke tells us that as he entered into Jerusalem, Jesus was crying too. He came as a king on a donkey as Zechariah 9:9 had predicted, yet he wept because the people there did not recognize the "things that make for peace."

The following day after Jesus walked into Jerusalem, the mood of the city would change. Many who welcomed him would soon cry, "Crucify him." The cross and the grave were before him. Yet he went forward. He did not hesitate or turn away. The fickle nature of the crowd was in stark contrast with the steadfastness of Jesus.

We face great challenges today. We feel led along by circumstances we cannot control. Interested to see what the news is, who the latest celebrity to contract the virus was, but scared to look at the news at the same time for fear that news of infection rates soaring, and the community fracturing, become more challenging than ever.

We don't feel at peace. Like Paul, we feel anxious. Scared. Uncertain about our health, our finances, about those we love.

Many of us feel we are confined. Confined in our homes. In our buildings. We are called to social distancing. What an oxymoron. How can distancing be social?

Paul writes that he was led by forces but was part of the procession of Jesus. This is where the peace comes. Not from us. This crisis is a reminder that we are mortal. We are dust and to dust we shall return. Yet the peace comes from being part of Christ's procession.

I feel I am like that crowd these days. Carried along. I am whiplashed between feeling confident and hopeful by progress towards a vaccine yet feeling discouraged and anxious too. The financial markets swing wildly. I have several friends who have tested positive for the virus. Some are doing well and some are suffering or have suffered greatly. I am challenged by this time.

Yet we receive the messages of this time. Our ultimate future does not include our houses, our 401ks or even our bodies. Our ultimate future lies on the path which Christ sets before us.

It is that knowledge that God is in charge and that as nerve-racking and confidence-wrecking as this time seems to be for us, our peace is found in the arms of Christ.

We feel confined. Yet what Jesus calls us to is to not be confined. He wants our spirits to break free and march spiritually with him, confident towards the future. To know that Good Friday leads to Easter.

We walk with Jesus. We may have a spiritual awakening as a result of this time.

Jesus brings us peace. He frees us from being confined.

Maybe this time will lead to a great spiritual awakening for our country and world. The church which emerges will not be the same as before. We cannot fully predict what the church will look like as a result of this. Yet we can hope there will be a spiritual awakening.

Who do we follow into that future?

In any parade there is someone who is honorary leader, as I mentioned. A politician or ministry person or band leader. Often called the Grand Marshal. Paul was not a Grand

Marshal. When he wrote to the Corinthians, he described himself as being a follower in a parade. In Roman times, when the Romans were victorious in battle, they would lead a military parade, and the vanquished would be at the very back. Writing to the Corinthians, Paul describes himself as being in the back of a parade led by God.

Luke tells us that Jesus' triumphant entry into Jerusalem was later followed by another parade. That after Jesus was tried and convicted before Pilate, he was led away by soldiers. Near the front of his own procession. Usually a prisoner such as Jesus would walk in a square of four Romans solders with a fifth soldier walking in front of him carrying a sign that detailed his crime. Luke doesn't mention any of that. Instead, Luke tells us several important details. That Simon of Cyrene was made to carry a cross behind Jesus. That a large number of people followed Jesus. That Jesus turned around to speak to them. He told them not to weep for him.

Luke would not include these details if they didn't matter. Luke leaves out the four soldiers around him or whether or not there was a solder in front of him. Luke does include that Jesus was not at the very back of the passion procession like Paul says a prisoner might be. Simon was behind him. A large number of followers were behind him. Paul says that God led the procession that he followed. Luke suggests some details and leaves out others to suggest that theologically, Jesus was at the front of his passion processional, with his followers behind.

Paul suggests that God leads the great procession. Jesus led this procession because he was God too. Fully God and fully human. He would walk the passion of the Via Delarosa to the cross. But as Paul was the follower in his parade behind God, so too Jesus' followers followed their God. Jesus led his followers. Not with a mace, but with a cross.

Like Paul, we are among the captives in Christ's triumphal procession which would have no end.

We need not weep for him for he is God, the leader of the pack, the Grand Marshal of the parade, fully God, who would go to his passion and beyond. Christ would lead a triumphant procession that would have no end. As anxious as Paul was, he was part of a processional of Christ, and nothing, no enemy or virus or isolation, nothing in the world could defeat it.

We are not confined but defined, freed, and led by Christ. The one who gives us peace.

These are anxious times. So, friends, as you follow Jesus Christ, leave a legacy by writing to the next generation and share your commitment.

God Will Be There for Each Generation

Let those who follow you know of your faith. Luke tells us that at different times when crowds gathered to listen to Jesus, he gave them examples of God's saving grace towards lost sheep, lost coins, and a human example, lost sons. Sometimes this last one is called the parable of the prodigal son. In it, a man had two sons. An older son who was dutiful and stayed on the family farm and a younger son who didn't. The younger son said to his father, "I want my share of the inheritance now." Amazingly, the father agreed and divided his assets and gave some to him. The younger son took his and traveled to a distant country. When things didn't work out there, he came to his senses and returned home. The "next generation" is always impulsive. Were we any different?

Sometimes we have to travel out in order to come home. As we grow up and become young adults, it can be in new locations and it is often in the questioning of things, including faith, that we end up coming home when we find our own identity in it. That is what the text means when the younger son, "comes to himself," after being away, and then returns home.

That is my own experience growing up Presbyterian but moving away from church and enjoying worshiping in Catholic and UCC and Baptist and Methodist and other congregations. They helped me feel stronger about my Presbyterian faith when I returned to it, finding both a spiritual and professional home in it.

The older son in the parable was upset, jealous, self-righteous about his younger brother. The older son had tried to live by the letter of the law but found no joy in doing so. Faith is not meant to be an obligation, but a celebration.

The older son in the story represents the self-righteous Pharisees and religious leaders who were criticizing Jesus for forgiving sinners and meeting with those on the outside.

In the parable of the prodigal son, the prodigal, the youngest son, leaves the home and the value system of his parents and gets involved in a variety of things. Yet in the end he returns home to be with his family. This is a story for every "next generation."

I would write to the next generation that no matter where you go in life and whatever challenges you face; you can always come home to God.

When we come to worship each Sunday, we are all reaffirming our baptismal covenant, reminding ourselves we belong to Christ and tapping into his power for the week to come.

What the father says at the end of the parable of the prodigal son is true. He tells the eldest son, "You are always with me." Indeed, we are always with God. And God with us.

It does not matter if you have moved around a lot or not. There is always a home of grace for you with God.

In spring 1984, I was confirmed as a Christian at Westminster Presbyterian Church in Ohio. In February of that year, I was well into the final stages of my confirmation journey, working on our statements of faith, preparing for confirmation Sunday. It just so happened that some friends of mine and I got tickets that month to see the British Pop Band, Duran Duran, for a February show in Cleveland, Ohio on their 7 and the Ragged Tiger tour. This was a busy time of year and we were trying to finish our confirmation statements but got a chance to take some time for the concert.

The show was on a Friday night. There was a massive snowstorm in Ohio that February Friday. It closed the schools, which rarely happened in my community. We had been hoping to drive up in the afternoon but there was no way we could with the snow. One of my friends started jokingly looking into renting a helicopter to take us from Dayton to Cleveland in the snowstorm. That was a terrible idea on many levels. So, we never made it to the concert. There was a lot of disappointment. We had to stay home and work on our confirmation statements of faith.

A couple of years ago it turns out Duran Duran performed at the Verizon Center in D.C. and so my wife and I and some friends went. It was a great reminder.

During the encore they sang a prayer for this who lost their lives in recent terror attacks, and rather than asking us all to raise our lighters as they would have in 1984, they asked us to raise our cell phones high, to spread the light as we would have on Christmas Eve.

It reminded me of writing my statement of faith, my letter to God, as a teenager, for confirmation, many years ago, in which I wrote about the light of Christ shining everywhere.

It's a reminder that there is grace in the world, everywhere. For even when things don't go our way or we fall apart from what we know, there is always hope of reunion.

Never give up on your faith. For God never gives us on us. God always wants to stay in relationship with us.

Follow Christ to Meet the Needs of the World

Many of us during this time are hurting. Many young people in particular. This could be a time to reach out in letter and action.

There is a famous song that goes, "Kumbaya my Lord, Kumbaya. Kumbaya my Lord, Kumbaya. Kumbaya my Lord Kumbaya. O Lord. Kumbaya."

Political agreement has become rare enough in Washington these days that when both sides agree the media often labels those situations "kumbaya moments."

The song Kumbaya has taken on cultural meaning. The song was big in the 1960s and 70's when groups like Peter Paul and Mary, the Weavers and Joan Baez recorded it. Many of us grew up singing it. As a boy, I can remember sitting around campfires at Cub Scout weekends or at camp in Michigan kicking back and singing Kumbaya with good friends. The idea of "sitting around singing Kumbaya" has become a metaphor for agreement and idyllic conditions.

Yet, in reality, these "kumbaya" moments are the opposite of what the song really meant. The history of the song is that "kumbaya" mispronounces an African America spiritual lyric. The words as they were originally written were, "come by here." Far from looking to idyllic conditions, Kumbaya was a written as a call on those who were ignoring injustice in the world, specifically in the rural south, to "come by here" and see the needs of the people. It was written to encourage people from the north to come and see the challenges of people's lives in Georgia and North Carolina in the 1920's. Or to come by here and experience the racial division and poverty in the Mississippi

Delta during the Great Depression of the 1930's and then to do something about it. Kumbaya, as it was originally written and sung, was serious and powerful. Not intended to create a sense of passive acquiescence or complacency, but to engage people in the reality of the lives of the poor.

I had a "come by here" moment at a different kind of campground a few years ago. On a very rainy night, I joined caseworkers in going to several homeless camps in northern Montgomery County to interview residents there.

We focused on two camps located behind White Flint Mall, really walking distance from our Presbytery offices. One in the woods behind a dental office and the other in the woods behind a railroad track and old car lot. We walked down mud paths to the tents and benches where residents congregated. I saw the clothes hanging to dry but became more wet from the rain. There in the woods, we slipped as we walked.

I went to help caseworkers interview residents for a local Vulnerability Index – a survey intended to determine which members of the community are most vulnerable to medical issues and, in the winter, environmental challenges like hypothermia. We sat on benches or in the tents, lit by flashlights, and asked people questions about medical history, employment, life, and ways of living. The residents know the workers and were happy to see us as we brought clean socks and some more lights. We asked them questions about how they got to be homeless. About how long they had been living there. Some had been living in the same camp more than five years.

It was a different perspective from my previous experiences with the homeless in New Haven soup kitchens. Or in Boston. In those cities, like in Bethesda, most of the homeless live alone, like those in our community at the bus station or metro. Through this experience I returned to my area of residence and began to get to know those in need in our area. The man outside the parking lot on Bethesda Avenue, or the brilliant, bi-polar fellow who sleeps on the park bench on Wisconsin Ave.

Things have gotten better in our area recently; there has been a reduction in homelessness in Bethesda in part because of concentrated work. Yet, at the North Montgomery County camps, where too many people remain, there is less mental illness, but criminal records are more common and there is more substance abuse than in the past.

I was deeply moved by the conversations. One man was born in south of Dayton, Ohio as I was. Yet different circumstances led us to different places, and we connected at the camp. Another man drinks a pint of hard alcohol a day. He had just finished when I talked with him. He seemed unaffected. One man, once a larger man, who was down to fewer than 80 pounds and was wasting away in his tent from liver disease. It was hard to intervene, but we needed to connect him with medical care.

One girl who I interviewed was born in 1992. She had three kids. When we asked where they were, she said with great sadness, "with my mother." Sadness that her addiction left her unable to care for her young children.

I had one man tell me that as a boy he wanted to be a preacher. At least his mother wanted him to be a preacher. He went to college for three years, now worked at a gas station and every other Saturday night he used the paycheck to buy a bag of powder cocaine. He lived in the camp as a result.

Most of the residents lacked insurance and their medical care came from emergency rooms. One man we interviewed had visited the ER seven times in the past month.

The sound of the train, so near, loud, and powerful it rattled the ground, raced by every 30 minutes. It makes it hard to talk let alone sleep.

Some people said they don't want help or to get out, but most did. Part of our response is to figure out who is the leader in the camps. If we can get the leader of the group to buy into the programs, the others would too.

Much of the key to their future is affordable housing. If people can get out of the tents and into housing, then they have incentive to find treatment, stay clean and perhaps find a job, because they don't want to lose the housing. Yet housing is expensive.

In many ways, the song Kumbaya is ultimately about the people asking God to come by here and help. That is what I saw during these experiences.

As the Bible omits much of Jesus' childhood, scholars debate whether Jesus' family was in the middle class in his day or poorer. We know his parents weren't rich, that Jesus was uninterested in achieving economic status and that Jesus called disciples largely from common trades. There is no doubt that Jesus was very concerned about the poor. There was little safety net in his day, and Jesus called those who would be fishers of people to concern for those who needed a net. In Matthew 25, Jesus said that when the Son of Man comes in his glory, he will divide people by on their response to the needy. "For I was hungry and you gave me food, I was thirsty and you gave me drink, I was a stranger and you welcomed me, I was naked and you gave me clothing, I was sick and you took care of me, I was in prison and you visited me." Then the righteous will answer him, "Lord, when was it . . .?' And the king will answer them, 'Truly I tell you, just as you did it to one of the least of these . . . you did it to me.'"

This virus has led to unprecedented economic pain. 36 million America filed for unemployed in just two months. More people out of work more quickly than almost any other time in US history. The stock market crashed, and many small businesses closed. Young people saw their careers starting on a difficult foot. Students missed critical skills as schools shut down. The next generation has a challenge.

The county I live in has 60K neighbors living under the federal poverty level, a large waiting list of families waiting for housing assistance, 1/3 of those impacted are children.

Each month people come to our church asking for money or for help to pay rent or utilities.

The prophet Micah famously wrote about what God requires of God's people. In his time, Micah was also concerned about conditions for the poor and justice in Israel. He suggested that Israel was failing in its responsibilities to its covenant with God. Israel and God were on opposite sides of what was a kind of trial. The hills and mountains, which had been present since the early days of creation and thus able to judge fidelity to the covenant, were slated to act us jury.

Micah concludes in his famous question about what God requires of us, that we should do justice, love kindness, or mercy as the King James Version puts it, and to walk humbly with our God. Nothing fancy. No attention-grabbing sacrifice. No great self-loathing, but simple compassion, decency, humility, and justice. Obeying God and loving neighbor.

Both Matthew and Micah set up kinds of trials for God's people. Eventually each of us will measure our lives or find them measured.

Remembering Jesus' words that it is important how we treat the "least of these," and Micah's statement about God's requirements of justice, love, and obedience, we think about our everyday walks with our creator and our attitudes towards each other.

As Micah suggests, God expresses deep emotions towards us. When we leave our comfort zone and are willing to "come by" where the needs are, in whatever way we do, we invoke deep emotions inside ourselves.

One Sunday a man, Charles, came to our 8:30 service. I know Charles. I know his background from the campground experiences. I know why he was there. He came for money and was happy to wait on the outside of the 8:30 prayer circle service until we were finished to ask for it. Instead, we invited him to join the circle. Charles lifted up a prayer in our circle. I asked him to come back during the week so we could talk. Frankly, usually when I suggest that people don't return. But Charles did. And we talked and cried and prayed together and stayed in mutual relationship.

Any church of Jesus Christ should be reminded that in Christ the divine "came by here" to see the needs of God's creation and through the Holy Spirit decided to stay and help.

Kumbaya my Lord, Kumbaya. Kumbaya my Lord, Kumbaya. Kumbaya my Lord Kumbaya. O Lord. Kumbaya.

Prayer as Action for Young People

How do we play a role in the continuing development and redemption of the world?

At the end of the famous biblical book of Job, after Job suffers a great deal, we read that the Lord "restored Job's fortunes and gave him twice as much as before." Yet God only does this after Job prays on behalf of his friends. These three friends who had made Job feel worse than before. God declares God is angry with them. Yet God says that if Job prays for them, God will not deal harshly with them. Job intercedes and prays for his tormenting friends to save them. Job helps redeem his part, his corner, of the world and God gives him even more than he had before he suffered.

We can relate our loss in the world to the role we can play in its redemption.

We can work for a society where there are supports for those who suffer.

This is what our denominational ecumenical advocacy days seek to do each year. This is what mothers who are part of MADD (mothers against drunk driving) do. This is what doctors and nurses facing Covid seek to do at hospitals across the country.

This is what young people who want to make a difference can do too. Many young people think they are not impacted by the Covid situation. Yet there can get sick. And young adults can stay home, wear marks, socially distance, for the well-being of others as well as themselves.

Young adults can make a difference. We saw that with young people and the Speak Up movement, a counseling and mental health opportunity for student-athletes across the country to talk about problems they might be having. With what the children and youth did after the Florida and Virginia Tech shootings. What young people around the country are doing with marches and actions for racial justice in 2020.

Our individual challenge is to find something in our corner of the world in which we can play some role in the redemption of the world.

Finding God Out in the World

Let the next generation know they can find God out in the world by being engaged in it. This is a hard time for the youngest generations just starting out. Yet they too can find God. Where is God? That is what the Israelites ultimately wanted to know on their wilderness journey. The book of Exodus tells us that in the wilderness, the Israelites asked, "Is the Lord among us or not?" This is often what we ask when we are anxious. When things are not going as we'd like. Is God here or not? Is God really with us? Where is God with us in this place? This is the question God's people have asked from Exodus to Job to the cross.

Matthew and Mark tell us Jesus asks the question on the cross of where God is when we feel forsaken and alone.

One Easter morning Mary came to the tomb and Jesus wasn't there. The tomb was empty. In the season of Easter, we affirm the words the angel tells Mary, "he is not here." Jesus is not here, but during this Covid-time, we are not here in the sanctuary either; we are not in our church. The message of this season is that Jesus is not where we expect him to be.

Friends don't look for Jesus in the church. He isn't here. Jesus appears to Mary and says, "Don't hold onto me," and "I'm going ahead." The angel says to Mary "go to Galilee, there you will see him." Don't look for Jesus in the church, for Jesus is out among us. Not only that, Jesus was out in front of us. We are called to go, go to him, follow him, go and do likewise.

You can't be in our building, well that is not where God is calling you to be anyway. You were never called to stay in the sanctuary. So, we are socially distancing, and we are home. Ok, but ministry happens in front of you, in creative ways.

In Exodus 17 God says to Moses "I am in front of you." So, "go." Twice God says "go" in the passage. Just like the followers of Jesus, the people of God in the wilderness are called to go. Go to where the holy is in front of them. There they will see God.

Is God among us or not? Yes, God is. God is with us. Not just here, but out there too. In front of us.

In front of you is a needy world. In front of you is a world where the crisis lays bare the injustices of the world. In front of you is a world of disproportional arrest and death rates. In front of you are the needs of millions of Americans filing for unemployment, and enterprises small and large shutting their doors. In front of you are parents struggling to do it all, students wondering what school will look like and seniors looking to know they are valued. In front of you the cries for more decency, unity, and leadership at the highest levels of government have never been louder. Out in front of you the importance of mending America's social fabric has never been stronger. We are called to find God amidst these troubles and help transform them for the better. To find and drink life-giving water from the hard rocks that confine us.

That part of our calling is to realize that Jesus feels deep and stacks high those things which afflict people in the world. That he calls us to feel the pain and injustice and challenges of the world in our time. Addressing them can help us find meaning.

We are at home with this viral separation, but we are called to think deeply about the needs of the world. Part of what can motivate us are our spiritual practices to help us find meaning in this time. To even write about how we might address those issues for the world.

Paul says that none of it can separate us from the love of God. But to stay close to God, we have to follow that God who lives in front of us and calls us to "go."

I served as a Bethesda Help "Officer of the Day" recently. That means taking calls from those in need in our area to help. This is a time for a record number of calls. The role of Bethesda Help involves helping to ensure food is delivered. One woman asked, could she have an extra giant card to buy cereal for her family.

I heard her voice in my head each morning that week as I cooked oats. When I got out cereal for my kids, I thought about this conversation. When we took groceries out of bags that week, I thought about that women. As I helped get something for lunch for my kids, I thought about that person. About living out the divine love Julia of Norwich wrote about, about being Christ's disciples by showing our love. About not forgetting those who feel left behind, but instead about our Christian work of delivering something like a parcel of cereal with a card of hope.

This Covid season a dry desert, a deserted tomb and an empty sanctuary tell us what is unique about this time. That God is among us, and out there, out in front of us. The promise of Easter is ahead of us. The message of Exodus is God is in front of us. The calling of our time is that we hear the words of scripture and realize that we are called to go find what we are looking for out there. That we may go forth into the season of grief to find a new perspective. A world where light and life and hope are found out there. To see God in acts of justice and love and kindness in addressing the needs of the world. That we are called to go out there to find what is holy. And in doing so to find ourselves.

When I went home this spring to see my parents, I knew I would be visiting my childhood home for the last time. I walked around the house and said goodbye to each room. I pictured my childhood adventures. The art show in the kids' bathroom. The rock concert on the porch. The picture of my sister in the living room. Sitting by the fires with friends and grandparents. Sleeping on the dog as a pillow on the landing. So many wonderful thoughts. As we drove away to the airport, knowing that when I returned next, I would not be visiting my childhood home again, I said goodbye to the house, and with it, to part of my childhood.

As I drove away from my childhood home, I was even more aware that I am now the parent, yet always still someone's child. And its alright.

Whatever it is for you, write to the next generation. To tell them about yourself, to shape them as you touch the future, and to call them to engagement in the world.

Prayer

Let us pray. Loving God help us to find sustenance during this time. To look with fresh perspective. To follow you out into the world. God, bring us closer to you. Help us to appreciate each other. Send us forth to play a role in repairing the world. Give us a word from you. Amen.

Chapter Seven
A Letter to Oneself

Life is a journey. It can be a long journey. It can be a short journey. It is a journey. Paul wrote in 2 Timothy, one of the final books he wrote, "I have fought the good fight, I have finished the race, I have kept the faith. Now there is in store for me the crown of righteousness, which the Lord, the righteous Judge, will award to me on that day—and not only to me, but also to all who have longed for his appearing."

Life can be really tough. It was tough for the Thessalonians and many of those Paul wrote to. Many churches had been persecuted, some people had been beaten, they were wondering at that time if the world was about to end.

We all want to live life well. To look back on life and think that we have lived it all. We want to be remembered for living life well. For having fought the good fight and finishing our race well.

We want to live by good virtues and the good deeds we want to be remembered by. How do we do that?

In writing a letter to ourselves, we can think about those questions and seek to answer them for ourselves. Perhaps to create an action plan. By reflecting inwardly and then committing to a set of values by which we want to live our lives and writing that on paper, we can move ourselves out into the world.

During this Covid-time, we may be able to write a letter to ourselves, to make sense of the wilderness we are in, and to emerge stronger from it.

Values

Cultural thinker and author David Brooks has famously, and wonderfully, written about two kinds of qualities – "resume virtues" and "eulogy virtues."[16] The first includes skills that help us in our usual work jobs, but the second includes values we hear lifted up at people's memorial services.[17] Brooks concludes that we know that the "eulogy virtues" are the more important.[18] The ancient Greeks believed in the importance of such values as well. Where do we develop the eulogy virtues? Brooks has many good thoughts on this as well in his books and articles.[19]

To me, they come from two places. First, from just having experiences. A wise friend at Bradley Hills calls it "time on earth." By the time we hit middle age, we start to shift our emphasis from the resume focus to the eulogy focus. I am there now age wise and see many friends focusing on values and virtues for the first time in unique ways. They have come to it because as we hit middle age, we begin to recognize our mortality in new ways. That causes us to pause, reflect, think about what is important.

The second way we develop the most coveted virtues is if something traumatic happens to us before middle age. A death of someone close to us. A loss or real struggle. Dealing with great adversity. All these experiences can force us to evaluate life and develop mature values more quickly.

---

16 David Brooks. "The Moral Bucket List." *New York Times.* April 11, 2015; from his wonderful book, *The Road to Character.* Random House. 2016.

17 Ibid.

18 Ibid.

19 Ibid.

This Covid time is providing examples to many of us. It is both threatening to us, which causes us to realize we are vulnerable and mortal. It is also providing a traumatic event, which is causing many to think about life and develop mature values for the first time. Adding to this the racial tension of our time makes this unusually important for us to think about what kind of culture we want to build and live in.

This is a wilderness time. Yet God uses wilderness journeys to develop values in us. In the New Testament, Paul took Timothy with him on some journeys. They were tested, threatened, and pushed during their trips. These trips caused Timothy to develop some values quickly.

In the Hebrew Bible, God led the Israelites in the wilderness in order to help, in part, them develop inner character and the values that it would need in the Promised Land. Wilderness experiences such as this Covid-time, can be times of growth.

The Wilderness Experience

Those of us in churches and beyond are in the exile of the wilderness. We are broadcasting virtually, working from home, doing school remotely, stuck outside of many of the things we value and enjoy. We are out of our usual routines. We are on a dark, disoriented, roundabout road, and even the experts cannot see exactly where it leads. Yet this is a chance to find God on the route, for all our roads can eventually lead us back to God. A God who also goes in front of us, into the future.

We are in the wilderness. The good news is that God's people have been there before. The Israelites knew what it was like to be in the wilderness of life as they fled from Egypt, a biblical metaphor for being outside of the usual parts of life.

How did the Israelites get to Egypt? From the end of the book of Genesis, we recall that Joseph's brothers got mad at him for being obnoxious and sold him into bondage. He eventually got sent to Egypt. Several years later there was a famine in Israel, and the Israelites traveled to Egypt to seek food. Their native son, Joseph, had prospered in Egypt and became sort of the COO of Egypt. He was able to help the Israelites when they arrived, and they did well at first in Egypt.

However, as they grew in numbers, the Israelites were seen as a threat to the Pharaoh and so he put them into bondage. He kept them busy working on infrastructure projects, including roads in northeast Egypt. Eventually, God sent plagues to Egypt to motivate Pharaoh to free them and that led to the people being let go. When the Israelites were granted freedom, they quickly left Egypt, taking the bones of Joseph with them. Our scriptures tell us they left so quickly they didn't have time to make provisions, so they ate unleavened bread. This is sort of where we were at the beginning of our wilderness experience in March with Covid, wasn't it? Many of us moved really quickly to get supplies and food and medicines to be ready to shelter in place.

When the Israelites left Egypt, many left from a place called Goshen. The area of northeast Egypt where the Israelites were confined was called Goshen which, in Hebrew, means "drawing near," as the Israelites were drawn nearer or closer to God during this period of time. They learned to rely on God when things were difficult in exile. We realize that part of our wilderness opportunity is to draw near to God as well.

Exodus tells us that there were several possible paths for the Israelites to take to get back to their Promised Land from Egypt.

The shorter route was called the "Way of the Philistines." That would have taken them north. It was a coastal path that moves close to the Mediterranean Sea. If you look at a map and trace your finger on it today it goes from around Cairo to around Tel Aviv. There would have been, then and today, a lot of people on it. Lots of places to stop. However, with lots of people there, they might have been attacked by robbers or inhabitants.

The second road was further to the south, all the way around the Sinai Peninsula. It was a dark, desert highway. An inland route like going out to a small rural road through the sand. In the Bible, it was called the "Way of the Wilderness." The road wasn't very good and there was not a lot of people nor water or food on the way. The sand would all start looking the same eventually and one could get lost. The Israelites got to see the sea, but their path would be just lots of desert. On a current map there were no great roads still.

Which one do you think God led the Israelites on? They had been preparing for the short, well-traveled path. Yet God sent them on the longer, harder road. It seems like God has a way of leading God's people on the harder routes in life at times. God sent the Israelites on the longer, harder road.

They were expecting to go the northeast route. It would be quick. They might be attacked. If they survived that early attack, they would make it to the Promised Land.

This is sort of where many of us are during this Coronavirus crisis. Many call this battle against Covid, a war. We thought perhaps we'd have a wave and then it would crest, and we'd have a quick vaccine and the world would be open for business soon and we'd be back in our sanctuary and to normal at work and school and life by Memorial Day 2020.

What we are realizing is this journey may be longer and harder than we had originally thought. Trying to reopen too soon risks a resurgence. We may be in the wilderness for a longer long time than planned. We may be out of our routines for longer than we imagined. Doctors tell us the vaccine may be a longer way off and social distancing will need to continue for a while. The economic impacts may be long-lasting. We may not all be back in our buildings soon. We may be walking in the wilderness for a while.

Yet there is some advantage to a long journey. The Israelites learned in their roundabout way how to journey with God. That made all the difference when they reached the Promised Land. They learned to walk with God. When you are disoriented, you are glad you have God to walk with in the wilderness.

On a long road like this Covid journey, we too may be able to develop some of the qualities we prize.

When one walks with God, one learns that God can be the one that helps us see more clearly, helps guide us, helps illuminate our paths on our dark, desert highways of life or disorientation. That God is always ahead of us.

Scripture reveals that God was with the people in the wilderness. They were in Goshen and God was with them. Moses had told them God would take notice of them. Exodus tells us God was with the Israelites leading them on the desert highway in the wilderness of Sinai. And it was dark.

God was with them in the darkness. Exodus expresses that God was with them in the light of the sky, the pillar of light, the light of the cloud by day and a pillar of fire by night, to give them light, so that they might travel by day and by night. This means the right amount of light. When you are walking in the desert at night you can get lost. God was light to illuminate their path. When you walk in the desert by day the sun is so bright its disorienting too as its blinding. Cloud cover helps provide shade which helps the people on the path. So, God appearing as light in the dark and cloud during the day was about being the right amount of light so the people could see. God stayed with the people to give them guidance along the path as they traveled day and night.

We don't like dark, roundabout journeys. We would prefer straight lines with predictable paths and well-illuminated roads. In the wilderness of the desert, all the miles of the sand look the same and one gets lost if they aren't careful. For us now during this Covid-time we can be lost to fear. Lost to anxiety. Lost to loneliness.

There is a reason darkness was the ninth plague that helped get the Israelites out of Egypt in the first place. We don't like the darkness. We feel vulnerable in the darkness. We can't see where we are going. We feel limited by the dark. Our vulnerabilities are magnified in the dark. We feel we get lost and can take the wrong, round about path.

Doctors and politicians and leaders and researchers don't know exactly where this wilderness time of Covid is going or when it's going to end. We can't see the exact path in front of us. We are in the dark. Our path is a roundabout journey as well through our desert. For the Israelites, their journey was the long route, the roundabout path through the desert. Life now is often a series of roundabout paths. We spend two hours in line just to get into Costco. We try and learn new skills in an economy that once seemed a straight line, but now seems confusing. Children try over and over to understand assignments. Teachers who were experts in their field try and become proficient at being online instructors if only the internet wouldn't keep crashing. We see someone in the aisle at a CVS or in our hallway and we walk the opposite direction. I find that dog walking is one big series of roundabout journeys as when we see people near us on the same path, we often walk far out of our way to avoid getting near anyone. Or we drive and drive around trying to find some store which sells toilet paper only to go in and walk around all the people and using seemingly as many tissues to open the door and pick up the container and hold our items and pay for the product as are in the package in the first place. We are on a long journey, a disorienting journey. We are in a round about time.

But God is not held back by the dark or the roundabout road. God is with us in the dark and on the roundabout path. God is with us in our dark, desert highways. Always in front of us.

Easter begins in darkness on a roundabout path. That is the way the women were on Easter morning. Getting up before dawn and making their way to the tomb. They couldn't quite see what was in front of them. It was so dark that Mary mistook Jesus for a gardener.

They were hurrying on a straight path to the tomb, only to be told be angels to take a roundabout journey. To then run out of their way to Peter and John and then again to other disciples, after going back to the tomb. Told by an angel to go to Galilee. Easter begins in darkness on an unexpected, roundabout path. Mary had run a straight line to the tomb, but in this Easter light, God led Mary on a roundabout path in the darkness of the first Easter morning. It was a path to Jesus and to redemption. In the early morning darkness, the only light, the right amount of light, was from God and it helped Mary to see. Dark, roundabout journeys can be holy too.

We have had many funerals put on hold during this time. Not long ago, however, I gathered with one of our church families at a cemetery. It was a bright day; the sun was shining, sharing very brightly, but inside us there was the darkness of grief. An unexpected death had cut short the life of a man who had beaten the odds only to have life ended early, and there was darkness felt. Moreover, where there normally would be hugs, there was roundabout distancing. Kisses on cheeks were replaced by masks, and people were apart for the service.

An armada of cars, with family members who usually would be sitting in rows of chairs around a casket, were lined in cars watching at a distance. I stood with a few family members under a tent that acted as a cloud from the bright sun in our eyes, so we could see each other more clearly as a computer connected us through Zoom with family members who would have liked to have been at the funeral if they had been allowed. This was a long, somewhat round about path to a burial service.

Yet when his son spoke, he spoke directly and clearly and light shown through him. He spoke in his own way. What I heard was about a beloved father. Directly about a father who loved him, had guided his path in life, and whom he loved. About a father who taught him a lot and would be missed. About a father who would still be with him in a way watching over him, like God watches over us, and right with him as a light shining as a lamp to his feet. I saw holiness there in that family.

We didn't choose the path we are all on. The Israelites didn't choose the roundabout path through the desert, yet it ultimately got them to the Promised Land. Mary didn't choose the roundabout path either. Yet that path took her to God. The Easter promise in the dark, disorientation of the morning, of the angel to Mary was, "go to Galilee, there you will see him."

It is the call and challenge to us now too. To ask ourselves on the dark, roundabout paths we are on now: Where have we seen God during this time?

Where have we seen the power of light overcome the power of night or disorientation or negativity?

Where have we seen the action of God overcome the action of death?

Where have we seen God in front of us?

Where have we seen God as light in front of us illuminating our paths?

Where have we seen God overhead shielding us from harm?

Where have we seen the spirit of God moving in mysterious ways, in the tears of loss and the joy of virtual hugs?

How has the light of God shown ahead of us in our grief and disappointment and displacement of this time?

Where has your life shown that Christ is risen indeed?

Where have you seen holiness?

In this wilderness time on this most unusual journey, God is with us. God is with us where we are. In the cloud and in the fire. In the apartment and in the retirement community. In the nursing space and the house. In the daylight and in the darkness. On the highway and in the home. On this dark, desert, disorienting journey. For the truth for any of God's people in exile and in the wilderness is the same as for God's people whether disoriented in the desert or depressed at an empty tomb - it's that God goes with us. Just where we are.

For God comes as light to us as well to illuminate the path in our disorientated wilderness so we can notice God day or night. Ahead of us on the journey.

It's a long road through this social distancing, but we walk it together. With confidence that the darkness will give way to light. That the roundabout way will reveal destination. That the confusion will give way to purpose. And if we keep walking it, we find that the dark, desert highway eventually leads to the Promised Land.

Realizing God is ahead of us and with us can be part of what we can communicate to ourselves, and that can give us strength of the spirit.

Journaling

As we seek to look inwards, to find God ahead of us during this wilderness time, this is a good time to write a letter to ourselves. I have found that writing regularly in a journal can be that letter.

As my parents got ready to move, as they cleaned out the house, they sent me several children's books from when my father was a child. I enjoyed reading our kids a copy of *Bambi* that my Dad received in February of 1944 with a handwritten note from his grandparents. They sent me some books on birds which were fun. They sent me a copy of *Rip Van Winkle* from 1941. *Rip Van Winkle* is a story by Washington Irving about a man who takes a nap and wakes up 20 years later.[20] He wonders what he has missed and finds out he has missed many things.

For many of us, we would like to forget this spring, and perhaps summer. Health crises, fever scares, job losses, social distancing, the deaths of people we care about, uncertainty about the future – this time has been a time like no other. Yet what if we had been like Rip and slept through it all? What is we had fallen sleep in February and woke up years from now? Rip missed some pretty significant things, including sleeping through the American Revolution.

If you met someone who had slept through this time, how would you describe this time to them? How would you describe this social distancing experience? This time at home with its isolation and challenges. Its burdens and blessings. Its isolations and oddities.

---

20 Washington Irving. *Rip Van Winkle*. 1819.

I personally have been trying to keep a journal of this time. Trying to write down my feelings and experiences of the days. I usually don't write enough. I'm an inconsistent journal-er at best. But I'm trying. I've encouraged my kids to write down reflections of this time. For this is history. Someday they will be asked about it and will be glad if they can remember back to this time. Writing a journal can be like writing a letter to yourself. It's worth trying.

How Will This Time Have Impacted Us as We Look Back?

This crisis has potential to make us kinder and more compassionate as a people or to accentuate our more selfish qualities. Which will it be? Facing death can help us to value life. Feeling vulnerable might cause us to focus on what is most important in life. I pray that God will resurrect our best attributes.

We are better off with others. However, not all of us can go outside at every moment and be social during this season. Being socially isolated is a major concern for many of us.

It is the case that something we cannot see now; a virus, is threatening us. We cannot deny science. Yet we should not deny our faith either. For it is also the case that the deeper values of things we cannot see, of the mystery of faith, can save us too, helping us to keep going through this time.

This Covid situation makes each of us think about the reality of our mortality. There is so much suffering during this time. How do we find God in it? Suffering can strip away our self-reliance and make us realize how much we rely on God's grace.

I have two friends nearing death as I write this. One of whom has beaten all sorts of odds. They are in the company of someone else from our family system now shuttling back and forth caring for them. So many of us, during this Covid time, are thinking about someone who is sick or died. It is a reminder that death comes to us all.

Let us write a letter to ourselves about how we can make this time one where we emerge showing our best selves. We can ask ourselves as we write, maybe in a journal, how does that recognition and remembrance that we are mortal change how we live? How does that make each day more precious for us?

We see God in the shadows, in the resilience of people, in the resilience of the human soul. Use the suffering and anger to walk along someone else and transform the world.

I went to see someone recently for healing. I asked them how they got to be so good at it. They told me they grew up as the child of missionaries in rural Papua New Guinea. They went through some real challenges during that experience. They suffered abuse. Now decades later they are still processing it. Yet their suffering gives them deeper resilience in their soul. It's the ability of someone with the scars of suffering to walk alongside someone else which they gained. Perhaps the resolution to walk along someone else will be our commitment of our letter to ourselves.

Committing to Change

Most of us don't like change. Most of us are creatures of habit and routine and are anxious about the changes of life. Humans are creatures of inertia. Congress has a stunningly low approval rating, yet we continue to elect the same people year after year with remarkably high rates of reelection for incumbents.

But part of the commitment we can make during this time is saying goodbye to part of the past.

As I mentioned, one of my favorite movies is *The Shawshank Redemption*.[21] In it, several of the characters, including Morgan Freeman's character Red, have trouble with change. They get so used to being in prison, where many of them had been for decades, that when they are released, they can't function outside prison. Freeman's character at one point while staring into a store, after being released, says, "I kept dreaming of ways to get caught doing things that would break my parole so I could be sent back to prison."[22] Sometimes we are so used to those things that hold us captive that we prefer that certainty to the unknowns of freedom. That was Israel's challenge in the wilderness too. They wanted to go back to what they were used to rather than embracing the future. This is where faith is key.

We would like to go back to the way things were before this coronavirus started. For the first couple of weeks of it in March, I kept waking up wondering if I had been having a dream and perhaps the dream was over. Now I have settled into the reality that this virus is here to stay in some form. We can't really go back. The situation is, for us, to stay the course. This virus will lead to something different.

The future of the church and culture and country will be different from the past. This is not an interruption, but a disruption. We need to be open to how it will be different. How we will need to change to be open to what the future looks like. We are leaving behind normalcy and regularity.

For the Israelites it took moving away from what they were used to in order to recognize how enslaved they were to a certain way of thinking. God opened their minds to the idea

---

21 *The Shawshank Redemption*. Directed by Frank Darabont, Castle Rock Entertainment, 1994. Film.

22 Ibid.

that change could be positive. That freedom was possible with God's help.

What about us? In faith, we too can be freed to think about what ills God can free us from. We have to unlearn certain habits before we can act like we belong in a Promised Land.

God called Moses to help put aside the water. Water is often a symbol in the Bible for chaos. It was in Genesis in the creation narrative and in the Noah story. It was in Job's tale and in John's story in Revelation 21. God is the master of chaos is one of the lessons of Moses parting the waters of the Red Sea. God worked through Moses to get the people to dry land like in the separation of sea and dry land in the creation narrative of Genesis. God worked through chaos, through Moses, to use the water to eliminate the threat of the attacking Egyptians. Much as the waters of baptism cleanse us from sin, water can help kill the virus, so keep washing your hands.

There are some who say we need to give up on social distancing now and head back to the way things were. I think there is some wisdom in having respect for where we are. How we might keep going into this new world. How we stay the course of healthy distancing.

This is a painful time. There are strong economic reasons to try and head back to where we were, but in the long run the economy will be strongest if we keep going in our wilderness a little longer, motivated by science and trying to keep up social distancing. We need to respect the virus, stay still, we need to be guided by science and, like the Israelites, to take responsibility to keep going.

In the midst of the chaos and challenge and that which can paralyze us, we must still our hearts to move forward. We must push aside that which is in our way to move forward into freedom, into hope, into our Promised Land. We can find a new way. We can choose a new way of living in the world. A new way of loving each other. A new way that doesn't return to the politic and personalities of division and being less than God has intended for us.

Perhaps it is a word of gratitude which makes the most difference for you. I sat with a woman recently from church we had counseled. She had a spouse and child both with challenges. We talked about writing down one bright moment each day. She has shared since then that that advice made a real difference for her.

Looking for bright moments, or to share a positive thought, can be part of what we write to ourselves. Diana Butler Bass suggests, "Psychologists and medical professionals recommend keeping a gratitude journal… as evidence mounts that writing about blessings reduces stress and improves moods."[23]

As I have tried versions of that myself, I can attest that it does help improve life's journey.

My parents moved houses during the time I wrote this piece. They sold their home. Then the virus hit. Then needed to move. Then at the end of that first month, they gave up my childhood home and moved into a new place. Trying to move after 45 years in a home in the middle of this pandemic was hard. I was there helping them as much as I can. It was not easy. Yet I can sense the joy from my parents in planning to have it done. Great joy. I am so proud of them for their decision despite inertia and dislike of change and fear. The result will be joy. There is joy to be found ahead of us. In getting to a new place through this time.

---

23 Diana Butler Bass. "When I Needed a Gratitude Intervention." *The Christian Century*. March 20, 2018. From her great book, *Grateful: The Transformative Power of Giving Thanks*. Harper One. 2018.

Despite this pandemic, there will be joyed to be found ahead of us.

A wise friend said recently, "Often the fear of letting go is harder and greater than what is actually missed."

Change is difficult. We prize our comforts, our idols, our memories, and our routines. So did the Israelites. But their dreams only came true, even if it took forty years, when they were still in their anxiety, trusted God rather than turning back, told themselves they could do it, and looked to the future.

Be willing to seek change out of this crisis. We have fears at this time, and they are well founded. Knowing God is in control and with us in our fears can make all the difference.

A few weeks before the pandemic started, I went back home again to Ohio. I walked through every room in the childhood house and said goodbye. Maybe during this time you might say goodbye to some things. Say goodbye, in order to move forward.

On Nov 4, 1956, Martin Luther King Jr. wrote imaginary letter pretending to be from the Apostle Paul.[24] It called for real racial justice and change. Perhaps we can seek to write today about the changes in our country that must be made in the inspiration of not only Paul, but of King as well.[25]

What are you committing to at this most unusual time? How can perhaps writing a letter to yourself, or series of

---

[24] Martin Luther King, Jr. "Paul's Letter to American Christians." Sermon. Delivered at Dexter Avenue Baptist Church, Montgomery, Alabama, on November 4, 1956. MLKP; https://kinginstitute.stanford.edu/king-papers/publications/knock-midnight-inspiration-great-sermons-reverend-martin-luther-king-jr-1.

[25] Ibid.

them in a journal, about what you are committing to do, help you on your journey? What can you write to affirm in yourself? What can you write to express gratitude to God? Write a letter to yourself. You deserve it.

Prayer

Loving God, help us to know we were created for something important and special. Help us to look up to the heavens. For that is where our help comes. Help us to hear your call and to follow you, our way, our truth, and our life. Amen.

Conclusion

These pages encourage Christians to write five letters. This Covid-retreat time where we are socially distant and separated from each other may be the right time to write letters as a spiritual practice. They could create purpose and action during this most anxious and unusual time.

Writing as an act of faith might reflect God's own actions. For the Bible is God's love letter to you. Holy scripture is a letter of God's love for you and me. John tells us that in "the beginning there was the word and the word was with God and the word was God." The creative process of God works through God's word. God spoke to ancient people and continues to speak to us still through that holy word. The Bible is the word of God written for you and for me.

Do Not be Afraid

This is an anxious and fearful time. We are scared by this new virus. Everyone is impacted by Covid 19. At first, we thought it was just an issue for people over a certain age. Now it seems each day the newspapers have some article about how younger people are impacted. There are many feeling vulnerable that aren't used to thinking of themselves as a vulnerable population.

There are some of us filling for PPP or loans or unemployment. We are all vulnerable and we aren't used to feeling vulnerable. More of us need healing than we realized. We are scared.

We may feel we are walking in the valley of the shadow of death through this crisis. That scares us. Yet the Psalmist answers that we need fear no evil, for God is with us. We shall dwell in the house of the Lord forever.

We are not the church gathered this year. We are the church 8 insecurity. Illness or death. Having a secret exposed. Having a chapter of life end. On one hand our fears help protect us and help us protect others. When our fears limit or confine us, they are debilitating. I find that the greatest mistakes I have made or temptations I have failed to resist are mostly related to some underlying fear I have. I eat may too many sweets when I am anxious. I am tempted to avoid going to the doctor when it's related to my fears about mortality. I am tempted to hold onto tightly to activities or things or people when I fear of loss of control.

Now imagine that you had to face all your greatest fears at one time. Or that you had to go through all those temptations that you really don't want to face all in a row. That is what many of us feel during this time of illness, distancing, strife, recession, and division.

Fear of the Lord

This Covid time is a time of challenge. Yet, the Bible has another kind of fear in it, fear of the Lord. That means to revere and respect God. To fear the Lord enough to face our anxious fears is the goal. Belief, faith, and fear of God are related. There is fear of what is behind us, such as the Egyptians chasing the Israelites which made the Israelites afraid. Then there is fear, or respect, of God in front of us, such as the hope we will be with Jesus after death, which can inspire us.

Sometimes, what we try and leave behind chases us. Maybe we can't stop thinking about a relationship that needs mending. Or a mistake that haunts us and keeps us looking backward. What we need to have is something to be with us on the way that is able to pull us forward. That is where God comes in. Moses asked the Israelites to have faith. To be scared, but not afraid. To trust. To stand firm. To stay the course. To not give up despite what was challenging. The assurance of God is that we don't move forward alone. God does God's work of salvation for and in us. That can mean God leads us. That can mean God is simply with us telling our souls to be still and to know that God is here, even during Covid.

We may not know where we are going with this viral time or how we will arrive home, but we can stay on the path because we know God is with us. To fear the Lord enough to face our fears.

The Book of Proverbs tells us, "Fear of the Lord is the beginning of wisdom." Proverbs are meant to be practical statements of advice for living. A version of the phrase, "Fear of the Lord" is included 28 times in the Bible. Job refers to it. The Psalmist praises it. St. Luke writes in Acts 9 that the churches in Judea, Galilee and Samaria grew in numbers because they lived in the fear of the Lord. In Philippians, we read we are to "work out our salvation with fear and trembling."

Attempts to understand the world fail without considering God. Especially at this time when a virus we cannot see is threatening us, we need God. How can we really understand the creation of the world without thinking about the one who created the world? How can we understand the meaning of life without considering the God who gives life and gives hope for it to continue after death? No wonder we are frustrated seeking answers to life's biggest questions when we seek to understand them without the knowledge that only flows from God.

I know well that my greatest mistakes in life often have occurred when I have sought to act without any fear, or respect, of God. When I act arrogantly, rashly, or selfishly.

Considering the ideas of God usually leads me to prayer and

that, if nothing else, calms me. When I make a calm decision, I tend to make my best decisions. When I make a hurried decision or make a rushed action, it is too often the wrong one.

I find that my better or best nature is reflected in decisions when I include God in my decision making. I am more myself when I act in the world out of respect for God. That should not surprise me. We often associate wisdom with experience in the world. Who has more experience with the world than God?

In C.S. Lewis' Narnia Chronicles, the Christ figure in the stories is represented by a lion named Aslan.[26] He is perhaps my favorite character in literature. In *The Lion, the Witch and the Wardrobe,* the young girl, Lucy, famously asks of and about Aslan, "Is he safe?"[27] To which the response comes, "No,…'course he's not safe…..but he is good."[28] Lions aren't safe, but they are worth respecting, even fearing. So is the Christian life. Not safe, but it's exciting for us to be following a God worth respecting, and one that is so good.

For it allows us to face our fears. God's love letter to us tells us over and over, "do not be afraid." We read about it in the Psalms and the prophets, and in God's statements to Abraham, Joseph, and Joshua. Paul writes that God has not given us a spirit of fear. At Advent we read that when an angel tells Zechariah not to be afraid of his wife's pregnancy and Joseph received the same message in a dream.

---

26 C.S. Lewis. *The Lion, the Witch, and the Wardrobe.* 1950; HarperCollins, 2002.

27 Ibid.

28 Ibid.

At Christmas angels appear to the shepherds watching over their fields by night and say, "Do not be afraid, I bring you good tidings of great joy."

At Easter, God comes with earthquakes and angels and exciting news that Jesus is alive, and yet the initial human reaction to all this divine activity is the same - fear. Within ten verses in some Gospel translations, there are four references to fear. Matthew tells us that the guards were afraid. The angel says to the two women named Mary, "Do not be afraid," implying that they were also fearful. Jesus then tells them not to fear as well.

In every truly difficult and in every truly divine situation in life there is some fear.

We know Franklin Roosevelt once famously told the nation to be courageous about facing fears saying, "The only thing we have to fear is fear itself." The women at the tomb found that when God enters our fears, it can transform them into courage.

So in this Covid time, we must keep moving forward, coming to see our fears face to face and then going into the mission work that confronts injustice, into worship, into glorifying God, into the peacemaking activities, into the relationship, into the healing, into spiritual practices. We must always move forward with divine courage.

It can take courage to live a spiritual life. It takes courage to follow Jesus. It takes courage to face this time with the virus. It can take courage to write our thoughts and feelings in letters. Yet God is with you and me.

So, go ahead and write. Write your five letters. It's not about perfect stationary. Many of the favorite letters that I have ever written were written to my wife on United Airlines napkins. I keep every letter my kids write. They are precious.

It's not about the handwriting. I have really bad handwriting. One of my colleagues, who has had more than their fair share of having to decipher it, has called my handwriting, "not difficult but deranged." I know I'm not alone in having one's handwriting grow worse as the years have gone on. Yet I feel like letter writing is something I should be doing.
Computers help, but handwriting letters is good too. There is something special about a handwritten letter.

Paul didn't have it all figured out. Yet he wrote his letters. It might be a spiritual practice for us too.

I have a drawer in my office and someday I will slowly depart the church I serve and look at all the letters, handwritten letters, from friends from the church, which I have collected there. Many people at the church are wonderful note writers, with beautiful handwriting. I do and will enjoy reading those special notes someday as I look back at ministry.

I hope that when I look back, on my letters to God, to my parents, to a significant person, to the next generation and to myself, I will feel more alive, spiritual, grateful, complete, whole and nearer to God as a result of having written them. Maybe you will too. May it be so. Amen.

CPSIA information can be obtained
at www.ICGtesting.com
Printed in the USA
LVHW080448080920
665308LV00018B/1334